Specifying

Specifying

BLACK WOMEN WRITING

THE AMERICAN EXPERIENCE

SUSAN WILLIS

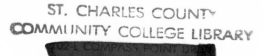
THE UNIVERSITY OF WISCONSIN PRESS

Published 1987

The University of Wisconsin Press
114 North Murray Street
Madison, Wisconsin 53715

The University of Wisconsin Press, Ltd.
1 Gower Street
London WC1E 6HA, England

Copyright © 1987
The Board of Regents of the University of Wisconsin System
All rights reserved

First printing

Printed in the United States of America

For LC CIP information see the colophon

ISBN 0-299-10890-2

In writing this book, I've had the help of:

Herb and *Tootie*, my parents in support
Hazel, my sister in endeavor
Gloria, my sister in conspiracy
Bill and *Edwina*, my comrades in life and politics
Fred, my mate in love and struggle
and my companions in spunk: *Justin*, *Cassie*, *Stacy*, *Cade*, and
Charlotte

I heard somebody, a woman's voice "specifying" up this line of houses from where I lived and asked who it was.

"Dat's Big Sweet" my landlady told me. "She got her foot up on somebody. Ain't she specifying?"

—Zora Neale Hurston, Dust Tracks on a Road

Contents

Specifying

1. Histories, Communities, and Sometimes Utopia

History gives topic and substance to black women's writing.[1] No one can read a novel by Toni Morrison or Alice Walker or Paule Marshall without confronting history, feeling its influence and experiencing the changes wrought by history. "They come from Mobile. Aiken. From Newport News. From Marietta. From Meridian."[2] Morrison's litany of place of necessity summons up the past. Culture, too, is synonymous with history. This is a body of writing devoted to the retrieval of Afro-American culture—the language, songs, poems, dance, stories, cuisine, and all the practices that shaped the daily lives of black people, so as to make these newly relevant for Afro-Americans of the eighties. Perhaps Marshall best underscores the function of history in black women's writing when the mother in her novel, *Brown Girl, Brownstones*, angrily asks her daughter, "But who put you so?"[3] All the novels by black women ask the same question. The answer to why Selina is the way she is, or why Sula is Sula, or why Meridian is Meridian involves reconstructing the development of the character's individual personality in relation to the historical forces that have shaped the migrations of her race, the struggles of her community, and the relationships that have developed within her family.

These are the most obvious ways that history enters black women's writing. But I would say the relationship of their work to history is even more essential and significant. The single most important aspect of the history of North America, indeed, one that defines the entire modern history of the Americas and has only reached its most advanced stage in the United States, is the transition from an agrarian to an urban society. It has been esti- mated that at the turn of the century a third of the labor force in the United States was involved in agrarian production. Today that figure has dwindled to less than 5 percent.[4] Such a change has tremendous implications when measured in economic terms. The effects are all the more profound when we consider the influence on human social relations and the formation of people's sensibilities and desires. This is the historical context and wellspring of American black women writers. I know of no other body of writing that so intimately partakes of the transfor- mation from rural to urban society or so cogently articulates the change in its content as well as its form. Why this is so can be explained once we clarify the historical terms of the transforma- tion as it relates to North America. Most economic theory on the subject has been shaped by the history of Europe where the movement of land-based workers to the cities has been repre- sented as a transformation in class from peasantry to industrial proletariat. The broad history of Europe is defined by the devel- opment of capitalism out of the previous feudal system. The problem with simply sliding the Americas into the European for- mula is that the post-Columbian world evolved under capital- ism.[5] Notwithstanding the manorial architecture and design of the hacienda, notwithstanding the aristocratic demeanor and style of the Southern planter, neither represented feudalism per se nor gave rise to a peasant population analogous to the Euro- pean model. Agricultural production in the New World was never based on a contract of production for protection, but rather on the dictates of a world market and the need to amass tremen- dous profits in the metropolis.

The defining instance of agrarian production in America is the plantation—not the freeholding, the slave—not the yeoman farmer. The fact that most Americans believe the reverse, seeing slavery as a purely Southern aberration, not representative of the real America, Midwest America, has a lot to do with the way history is traditionally told from the dominant point of view. In this case, the interests of capitalism are better served if one overlooks the great inequalities of the system, whose primary form of labor control in the New World was slavery, and imagines all workers as free individuals who "sell" their labor power on the open market. As capitalist ideology would have it, the yeoman farmer is the rural equivalent of the industrial proletariat.

The fact is that before the Civil War roughly half of the agrarian labor force was enslaved, and after Emancipation up to the early 1900s much of the agrarian population (both black and white) continued to be bound by the system of debt peonage known as sharecropping. For these reasons, the notion of a rural peasantry does not fit the American reality; so too, for reasons arising out of the marginality of the American rural underclass, it is erroneous to equate migration to the city with a process of proletarianization. Although many forsook the rigors of sharecropping for the hope of a better life up North, not all attained Henry Ford's promise of full employment and five dollars a day. Far more black immigrants than white have discovered that the city is another name for a sporadically employed labor pool. For this reason, urbanization, rather than proletarianization, would be a better way to characterize the history of the transformation from a land-based to an industrial-based economy in North America.

Thus, American history might be better understood from a point of view that has traditionally been seen as a minority position and an economics traditionally defined as marginal or aberrant. But this does not necessarily explain why black women might have a better grasp of history nor why their fiction might better articulate historical change. The black woman's relation to history is first of all a relationship to mother and grandmother. In interviews, Paule Marshall has stressed the influence of her mother's kitchen community on her writing. As a young child growing up in New York, she, like Selena in her novel, would hear her mother and neighbors talk of their Barbadian past while preparing island food. In their accents and conversation they created a cultural context that would later be the source of Marshall's access to the past. Similarly, Alice Walker's book of essays, *In Search of Our Mothers' Gardens*, is devoted to revealing the influence of mothers—both in the flesh and in spirit—on the formation of a black woman's creativity. Recognizing her mother's flower garden as her "art," Walker ponders the subtle (and subversive) ways black women have worked to inspire their daughters and wonders what sort of traces Phyllis Wheatley's mother could have left on her daughter's writing.[6] For black women, history is a bridge defined along motherlines. It begins with a woman's particular genealogy and fans out to include all the female culture heroes, like the folk curers and shamans known as root workers and Obeah women, as well as political activists like Sojourner Truth and Ida B. Wells who have shaped the process and marked the periods of black history. If the present is defined by the city and the North, the past is the South or the more distant Caribbean. Journeying on motherlines gives access to the geography of migration.

While interest in their mothers' and grandmothers' generations gives black women writers access to the past, there are economic and historical reasons why black women are in a better position to grasp history as a concrete experience. The history of black women in this country is the history of a labor force. Almost every black woman living in the United States has as her past the accumulated work of all her female forebears. This is not a generalization. Only recently, with the advent of wage labor, have some black women, the wives of fully employed factory workers, enjoyed interludes of respite from labor. And only now, with the existence of a black bourgeoisie, might it be said that there are some black women in this country who have not worked outside the home for pay. As workers, black women shaped their present and intimately knew the circumstances of their moment in history. Because the mode of labor defines the epochs of history; black women have had firsthand knowledge of slavery, sharecropping, and domestic and wage labor.

But the relationship of black women to history is twofold. As mothers, the reproducers of the labor force, black women have had a keen awareness of history as change. In their hope for their children's future, black women have learned to be attentive to moments of historical transition and many have struggled for social change. In their role as producers, black women have known the present; then, in relation to the economics of reproduction, they have envisioned and strived for the future. As workers, they have sustained their families; as mothers, they have borne the oral histories from their grandmothers to their children. For all these reasons, today's black women writers understand history both as period and as process. Certainly this is the lesson of Alice Walker's great historical novel, *The Third Life of Grange Copeland*,[7] whose definition of historical modes and movements defines a conceptualization of history sadly lacking in American schools.

There are many ways that history enters black women's fiction. The most obvious has to do with the way a character's journey enacts the migrations of the race over many generations. This is the case for Grange Copeland, whose journey from South to North embodies the labor migrations for many twentieth-century black Americans to the industrial cities. Journey as metaphor for migration also structures Toni Morrison's *Song of Solomon*, in which Milkman's quest into the South retraces in reverse fashion the migrations of black people from Africa, to the plantations, and then to the Northern cities. Similarly, Paule Marshall's Avey Johnson journeys to the Caribbean to create a bridge to her people's past. In all these novels, the individual's story and experience express the untold histories of black Americans. And in all these cases, geography serves as a means for conceptualizing history either as a specific mode, when it is crystallized in a place such as Morrison's description of

Shalimar, or as process, when it is experienced as the duration of journey.

The relationship that obtains in black women's fiction between South and North, or between Caribbean island and Northern metropolis, or between Africa and the United States defines history as economic modes. The portrayal of the South is not backdrop, local color, or nostalgia, but precise delineation of the agrarian mode of production. Similarly, the Northern metropolis is depicted as the site of wage labor and the politics of class. Journey North is felt as the transition between two modes existing simultaneously within capitalism, but the one—the agrarian mode—is destined to pass out of existence.

Black women writers portray the difference between South and North as a difference in economics. Specifically I'll cite Toni Morrison, whose writing is the most metaphorical of today's black women authors and therefore less likely to be apprehended in an economic sense than by comparison to a writer whose references to economics are more explicit, such as Alice Walker. I will also refer to a brief incidental episode in one of Morrison's novels, one not highlighted in the text and certainly not the subject of any critical attention. In this way, I hope to demonstrate just how pervasive economic concerns are and how profound the author's understanding.

The incident occurs in *The Bluest Eye* and takes place in an upstairs apartment occupied by three prostitutes. Here, among the curling irons and bras, the child, Pecola, sits listening to the women's chatter. Out of the banter and gossip, an anecdote begins to emerge, which, for its combination of simplicity and sensuality, cannot help but delight the reader and certainly captures Pecola's attention. A product of the city, the child of a sometimes-employed, alcoholic father and a battered mother whose work as a domestic sustains the family, Pecola will never experience the mode of life she glimpses in Miss Marie's account of eating fried fish with her boyfriend. For Pecola, born in the city's lumpen, and Marie, the urbanized immigrant, the episode depicts a mode of life so different from their present situations as to be the food for utopian fantasy. It is significant that nothing in the anecdote suggests wage labor or even the need for money. This is remarkable since neither Marie nor Pecola are themselves wage earners, but depend for food, clothing, and housing on the fluctuating employment of the men in their lives.

> "Every Saturday we'd get a case of beer and fry up some fish. We'd fry it in meal and egg batter, you know, and when it was all brown and crisp—not hard, though—we'd break open that cold beer. . . " Marie's eyes went soft as the memory of just such a meal sometime, somewhere transfixed her. All her stories were subject to breaking down at descriptions of food. Pecola saw Marie's teeth settling down into the back of crisp sea bass; saw the fat fingers putting back into her mouth tiny flakes of white, hot meat that had escaped from her lips; she heard the "pop" of the beer-bottle cap; smelled the acridness of the first stream of vapor; felt the cold beeriness hit the tongue. (*TBE,* 46)

I want to argue that even though the incident takes place in Chicago, Marie's account of the fish fry is a metaphoric representation of the Southern economy. This is possible because of the economic connotations associated with fish. In the black cultural tradition, "goin' fishin'," fish tales and fish fries commonly suggest "time off" and the procuring of food by alternative economic means. In fact, throughout American popular culture fishing is often represented as a contestation of private property. Anyone who has grown up on Saturday cartoons and "The Little Rascals" knows that a "NO FISHING" sign is an invitation to hook and line.

The succulent fish, the oil dripping down fingers and mouth, the crunch of fried batter and bone—Morrison's description exemplifies her use of sensual detail to give shape to the opposite of a wage-labor economy that she invariably situates in a residual image of the South. The anecdote offers an alternative to wage labor and industrial alienation, it matters little that the real

South was equally oppressive of black people. In fact, the real South has been transcended in the making of a metaphoric memory. The function of the anecdote is to generate the notion of alternative possibilities, not to conjure up a purely nostalgic image of the past and the South. The question at the heart of Morrison's fish tale is: don't we all have a right to experience pleasurable gratification in our daily lives? Given the contradictions and inequalities of capitalism, this is an extremely radical notion.

The South in contemporary black women's fiction is never portrayed as even a partial wage-labor economy, even though many Southerners have worked for a wage, particularly during this century, and a percentage of these have been black. What black women are documenting in the writing is the essential characteristic of the system as a whole as it arose out of slavery. In his book *Blues People*,[8] LeRoi Jones (Amiri Baraka) comments that emancipation signaled the instantaneous need for an entire population of black people to seek a wage. The Southern economy, conditioned by the history of slavery, engendered a number of labor strategies, which, like sharecropping and the labor camps documented in Hurston's *Mules and Men*, bound black people to the land either as farmers or as the primary extractors of raw materials. The pattern of paternalistic domination was continued through a system of debt peonage. This greatly influences the way work is conceptualized. For the laborers in Hurston's portrayal of Florida's turpentine camps, work was clearly something you did because the straw boss (a twentieth-century equivalent of the overseer) told you to do it. An antithetical, although similarly nonwage-labor attitude toward work informs one of Hurston's novels, *Their Eyes Were Watching God*, in which work is depicted as a pleasurable communal experience. One book shows the reality of Southern agrarian labor and the other exemplifies its utopian antithesis, but neither version articulates a sense of work as it is perceived in a wage-labor economy, where the worker trades his or her labor power for the sake of the weekly paycheck. At the heart of wage labor is the notion—no matter how false—of accumulation. If the capitalist turns surplus value back into capital and investments, the laborer ekes out the purchase price of a TV, car, or house. This is the tragic lesson Paule Marshall brings home to the reader in *Brown Girl, Brownstones,* where the transformation from tenant farmer to urban worker is marked by the obsession to "buy house"[9] out of the painfully accumulated nickels and dimes saved from the week's pay. Going North is, then, a metaphor for the transformation from peonage to worker alienation.

I'd like to return to Morrison's fish fry and take up the question Pecola poses to break Miss Marie's spellbinding account of fish and beer:

"But what about the money?" (*TBE*, 46)

Although Pecola's question is generated out of her recognition of dependency in an economy defined by the possession of money, Morrison is also directing our attention to a very interesting aspect of the Southern agrarian economy and the way it is remembered. As a nonwage-labor economy, the South is very often depicted as a nonmoney economy. This is a typical feature of sharecropping—a whole year's work can be computed in the pages of a book and translated into plow lines and seed in the spring, clothes and supplies in the fall. The ledgers that comprise the secret narrative of Faulkner's story "The Bear" testify to the paucity of exchange involving money and the brisk transaction in human lives and emotions that evolved on the plantation and were handed down to the sharecropping system. Of course, there was real money in the South, tremendous fortunes made and lost, great profits made and squandered. But the money existed at the top, even more so than it has in the industrial North where wage labor allows a pittance to filter into the hands of its employees. In black women's writing about the South, money is never perceived as a fact of life as it is in the proletarian novel where weekly or monthly regularity makes it the worker's vitamin pill. Rather, it very seldom enters people's lives and when it does it comes by way of marginal endeavors like gambling and bootlegging. Hurston's portrayal of Tea Cake, who works in Florida's bean fields but fills his pockets as a gambler, is the Southern antecedent of Miss Marie's Chicago boyfriend. Historically, gambling and bootlegging have afforded black men the opportunity to deal in a money economy without being employed by the economy. In black women's novels these endeavors are transformed out of the grim reality of marginality and dependency and become instead metaphoric statements of alternative economics not incorporated within capitalism.

Perhaps the most fully evolved sense of an alternative economics occurs in *Song of Solomon*.[10] Here, the contrast Morrison develops between Macon Dead and his sister, Pilate, is rooted in real history and demonstrates the development of urban capitalism in relation to its marginal agrarian economy. History follows the trajectory of Macon's life and immigration from the land he remembers farming with his father to Detroit where he rakes in his tenants' rent payments. Macon exemplifies the inception of the black bourgeoisie, whose class status is based, not on big business, but on the professionals and land speculators who are the allies of business. If Macon's development represents the course of real history, his sister's life embodies its utopian transformation. Although Macon and Pilate derive from the same African progenitor and are nurtured in the same rural economy, Macon, as the male heir, is destined for acceptance into capitalism's history, but Pilate, the woman, is marginal. But what's truly significant about Pilate is that she does not simply represent the rural South as the antithesis of her brother's development. Rather, she embodies the transformation of certain aspects present in the agrarian economy but not allowed to come to fruition in the real history of the South because of its larger economic domination by the industrial economy. Pilate is the realization of the communal and nonaccumulative aspects of the rural economy. Her household is devoted to the pleasurable incorporation of work into daily life. Money enters the household not to be hoarded up but to facilitate giftgiving, wine making, and the balanced flow between economic and human needs. The novel demonstrates just how thoroughly Pilate represents the transcendence of the rural economy when Milkman journeys south to a real agrarian community: Shalimar. Workers in Shalimar assemble before dawn waiting to be shipped to distant farms where they will make a day's substandard wage. The relationships between men and women in Shalimar are more apt to be defined by rivalry than sharing, and anything new or foreign will be viewed with suspicion. In a situation of economic dependency, the lack of accumulation and the economic necessity for communal living are the tangible features of oppression. Pilate lifts these features out of the real economics of the South and brings an alternative economic and social model into being. In her portrayal of Pilate, Morrison asks us to imagine a very different history of the United States, one that might have generated a community much larger than a household. The agrarian system capable of producing such a society could not have evolved under capitalism. If Pilate gives shape to the utopian imagination, she does so in relation to the industrial North and the agrarian South as these have *both* been shaped by capitalism.

I want to move now from considerations of content to form. Clearly, black women writers' sensitivity to history is all the more striking in their development of narrative modes. Just as history is what the novels are about so, too, is it embodied in how the novels tell their stories.

In considering narrative form and its relationship to historical modes, I first of all want to urge the reader to abandon any overly pat notion of history as a chronology. Although rural society might be thought of as being prior to industrial society, both forms have existed simultaneously as halves of capitalism's whole in the New World. Similarly, although a particular writer might be more closely associated with a particular narrative form, the writers are themselves living in two worlds and in touch with both urban and agrarian modes. Early in this century, Zora Neale Hurston already exemplified the dual influence of North and South on her work.

The best way to begin to define the formal characteristics of contemporary black women's writing is to conceive loosely of an overall development from agrarian to urban, but to realize that all the writers as well as the body of their writing embrace the whole of the twentieth century as a period of transition with great variety and inequalities existing side by side. Although a particular narrative mode might predominate in a writer, all the writers will give evidence of all the formal possibilities here defined. For example, I think all of us who have read a number of books by today's black women have noticed what I call the "four-page formula." That is, most of the novels seem to be compiled out of short pieces of writing. This is obviously the case for Morrison's *Sula* and *The Bluest Eye*, in which all the characters and situations seem to be given as pieces lifted out of some much larger narrative continuity. The situation is roughly the same for Walker's *The Color Purple* whose letter-writing format easily conforms with the brief form. Even *Meridian*, which gives an overall impression of narrative totality, is in its opening chapters comprised of short anecdotes. Essentially, the "four-page formula" embodies the storytelling tradition. It shapes Toni Cade Bambara's development of the short story as well as Morrison's version of the novel. The "four-page formula" establishes a teller-listener relationship between author and reader that doesn't necessarily pertain to other examples of contemporary American fiction. In this, black women's writing fundamentally departs from the mainstream of the bourgeois tradition, whose novels presuppose a sustained and leisurely reading; it equally diverges from the postmodern, Robbe-Grillet-type novel, whose narrative bits represent sundering and fragmentation rather than the narrative closure of the four-page anecdote. The "four-page formula," although longer than most of the Southern folktales related in Hurston's *Mules and Men*, is not so long that it can't make up a bus-stop or telephone conversation. A novel based on the "four-page formula" partakes of the rhythm of daily life as it evolved in an oral agrarian culture.

The strongest influence on the development of black women's narratives derives from the storytelling tradition. As it emerges in Hurston's collection, storytelling in the American South is very different from the tradition that evolved under European feudalism. First of all, there is no storytelling master, no single poet-orator as we might imagine the teller of the *Cantar de Mio Cid*. Such a storyteller would have been chosen for special gifts of memory retention and rhythm. The storyteller and the tale would have to be pleasing to king and commoner alike and the storyteller would have occupied a position of privilege in society. In contrast, everyone in the Southern black community participates in storytelling and story listening. Although certain individuals might give a better rendition of a particular story or might be better endowed as narrators, no one is excluded from telling or denied an audience. Women tell tales equal to men and children as well as the elderly participate. Instead of an individual storyteller occupying a position of privilege, history and the cultural tradition are privileged, as these are the lifeblood and spirit of the community. Furthermore, there is no separation between teller and text. Rather, the speaking subject is at one with the narrative, as are the listeners.

Before demonstrating how the storytelling tradition is felt in contemporary narrative (aside from the "four-page formula"), I'd like to focus on another facet of oral society as it will enhance our understanding of the oral narrative as a formal mode. In *Dust Tracks on a Road*, Hurston draws the striking picture of a woman "specifying" against a fellow camp worker. Her foot up on her neighbor's porch, Big Sweet unleashes every barnyard epithet in her repertoire including the assention that "his pa was a double-humpted camel and his ma was a grass-gut cow."[11] The practice of "specifying," or name-calling, exemplifies many of the formal features of storytelling as well as some modifications that are important for the development of the narrative. Although name-calling unites the speaking subject and the community, it does so at the expense of the individual being made the object of the abuse. The community is no longer defined as a corpus of teller-listeners, but as witnesses to the textual event. The position of the speaking subject has become marked and, to a degree, isolated. All the terms of the narrative equation have been modified; these modifications begin to suggest the sort of changes produced when the speaking subject becomes an author and the text a novel. Still, "specifying" preserves one aspect of storytelling intact: Just as there is a direct relationship between history and community, just as the meaning of stories includes the meaning of the group, so too does "specifying" insist on a direct relationship between the names and the person being named. The only thing that stands between the signified and the signifier is the name-caller who gives herself as guarantor of the relationship, with the whole community standing witness to the contract. "Specifying" represents a form of narrative integrity. Historically, it speaks for a noncommodified relationship to language, a time when the slippage between words and meaning would not have obtained or been tolerated. Such concerns are important in contemporary black women's writing, as I will show in the discussion of Toni Cade Bambara's "Gorilla, My Love" (see chapter 6), whose young protagonist rebels precisely against the sort of schism between signified and signifier that not only typifies the narratives and theories generated under late capitalism, but also serves the interests of domination.

Another striking example of how the oral tradition shapes contemporary narrative form occurs in Paule Marshall's *Brown Girl, Brownstones*. As a Barbadian immigrant, Marshall has in her background the tone and rhythm of dialect speech, which she reproduces at certain moments in the book, such as kitchen gatherings and weddings, to give voice and presence to the community. In addition, Marshall has developed a narrative modification of direct dialect in the vocal epithets that introduce many of the novel's chapters. Thus, the voice of the mother echoes through the house:

> "But look at he. Tha's one man don know his own mind. He's always looking for something big and praying hard not to find it." (*BGB*, 21)

Criticizing husband here, neighbor and roomers elsewhere, Silla's condemnations reproduce many aspects of "specifying." However, rather than the figure and voice of Big Sweet, Marshall's narrative adaptation embodies her speaker's voice alone. The community of witnesses, too, has undergone narrative erasure even though the epithets suggest a listening ear—a mute body of household listeners. The difference between "specifying" in Hurston's account and "specifying" as it occurs in Marshall's novel is the difference between a social form and a narrative form. The latter has its origin in the social and recalls for the reader the historical context of its formation, but, as a narrative form, it enjoys a degree of textual independence. These vocal epithets, like the lines from blues tunes and Harlem Renaissance poetry also incorporated into the novel, are recontextualized to give shape to a future tradition and culture whose content is built out of narrative bits.

Much of what I have said so far about storytellers and listeners as the defining mode of agrarian society might also be said with reference to song. Furthermore, it is in the black music tradition that we are best able to see the transition from an agrarian to an urban mode, and at the same time suggest some important parallels with the written narrative. The musical equivalent of storytelling is the plantation work song, which is based on a similar relationship between the singing subject and the body of participants that defines the storytelling community. Although there is very often a lead singer and a body of respondents, the song as text serves to unite the participants as a plural body. The notion of an individual artist is submerged in the music; what's heard is the song. Text and voice are one. All are singers; all are listeners.

As in Africa, where drumming evolved as a system of communication, the Afro-American work song also involves complicated rhythmic patterns. This, combined with the antiphonal singing technique, makes black folk music a multidimensional form. These are the formal features that are further developed in the transition to urban society where the folk form gives way to jazz. And I feel these same formal features suggest links between the musical text and the development of narrative forms. LeRoi Jones has stated: "Blues playing is the closest imitation of the human voice of any music I've heard."[12] If there is already a close relationship between music and the speaking subject, why not write voices patterned on jazz music? This is precisely what Toni Cade Bambara may have done in composing the many-layered and many-voiced communal conversations that occur in the novel *The Salt Eaters*. Certainly, complicated rhythm and antiphony hold much potential for the modern novel. But more than specific points of contact between jazz music and writing, I feel the development of jazz allows us to grasp larger considerations bearing on narrative and the black novel. As LeRoi Jones defines it, jazz occurs when black music attains a purely instrumentalized form, using, he emphasizes, European instruments. As such, it is the embodiment of the urban. It is the technology of the metropolis welded to the basic formal structure of African and Afro-American music. Jones does not define an evolutionary line from work song to blues to jazz, but like our definition of narrative forms, he sees each representing particular moments in a history in transition, each capable of influencing the other but not becoming the other. Likewise, Hurston's folktales did not become the "four-page formula"; rather, the modern narrative has the same rhythm, desire for closure, and relationship between teller and listener (in this case, writer and reader) as previously existed in the work camps and on the plantation. The "four-page formula," like Marshall's vocal epithets, may suit the format of the modern novel and conform with the technology of book publication, but they embody nonmetropolitan forms as well.

The special relationship between the speaking, or singing, subject and the community of listener-participants has an important bearing on a claim I want to make regarding black women as authors and their novels as texts. Throughout the history of Afro-American music and narrative, one might point to something of a tension between the emergence of individual speakers and the body of listeners or respondents. Various forms and various moments in history have allowed a greater differentiation of the individual: the "specifying" subject, the blues artist, the jazz musician, the author. However, the definition of the subject as an individual occurs only when we see the producer of black culture through the filter of Western bourgeois tradition. From this point of view, we fail to recognize the significance of the text, which is not just a song, story, or novel, not just another commodity to be used up and forgotten, but the embodiment of a community's relationship to history.

There is, however, one very great difference between the narrative forms that pertain to a properly agrarian society and those that evolved in urban conditions. Although folk forms are based on the presence of the speaking subject, which lends the text immediacy and guarantees narrative integrity, the transition to the urban involves the erasure of the speaking subject. Paule Marshall's Silla is a strong and vengefully resourceful woman, but she becomes, in the narrative epithets, a disembodied voice echoing through the house. Finally, with Toni Morrison's novels, we no longer have even the hollowed-out narrative reminders of Hurston's Big Sweet, but the text itself, a plurality of stories, none of them articulated by speaking subjects, but each one seeming to have a concrete reality all its own. It has become fashionable today to define everything as a text: history is a text; daily life is a text. Texts seem to take on a life of their own. I want to make a few critical observations about Toni Morrison's novels as texts because, although it's true these best exemplify the transition to the urban form as manifested by the loss of the speaking subject, they achieve an important, perhaps more profound, understanding of history than might obtain if the personalized agrarian form were simply updated to suit city tastes.

Earlier, I characterized Morrison as the most metaphorical of the black women writers. The narrative form that best expresses the urban as it is produced in relation to a dependent agrarian economy is based on metaphor. In considering metaphor, an essential question arises: if the speaking subject stood as guarantor of the relationship between signified and signifier, what happens to meaning once this relationship is replaced by larger narrative metaphors? Name-calling suggests a direct reciprocity between the name and its object, and the metaphor does have its roots in naming. However, metaphors like Morrison's fish fry substitute extended, sometimes highly condensed, and always multidimensional images for their referents.

The fish fry describes an allegorical relationship to history and suggests the importance of a fuller understanding of allegory in American fiction, one not bound by the rigid relationship between image and hidden meaning usually ascribed, for example, to Hawthorne. George Lamming, a leading artist-intellectual from the Caribbean, once remarked that he felt all his novels were in some way allegorical, and I think he would agree that the great majority of modern Third World writing is allegorical.[13] Indeed, Fredric Jameson has written on the allegorical relationship to history in the work of Sembène Ousmane and Lu Xun.[14] Metaphor and allegory best express the tensions arising out of periods of historical transition that have characterized Third World history from the era of discovery and conquest, through colonization and now more complicated forms of domination.

What's at stake in the use of narrative metaphor is not the particular relationship of a specific signifier to its signified, but the whole of the metaphor to the history whose meaning it allegorically evokes. Once the particularity of signification is no longer in question, the articulation of contradiction emerges as the crux of the narrative. This is true of politically conservative writers as well as the most progressive precisely because meaning is not dependent on a particular speaking subject but arises out of the text itself. This is not to say that the text takes on a life of its own, but rather the text whose mode of articulating history is based on metaphor captures the complex meanings and contradictory relationships generated by capitalism. This is possible because metaphor, based on condensation, delights in defining similarity out of contraries; whereas metonomy, which links contiguous categories, suggests the flow of continuity and cannot produce the distancing necessary for critical scrutiny that is possible in metaphorical relationships.

I am expanding on Freud's definition of condensation as he developed it in the course of his interpretation of dreams and their structure.[15] As Freud saw it, "dream-thoughts" (the images we remember upon awakening) are few by comparison to the great body of meaning these represent. The translation of extensive material into concise images requires "condensation" and produces a metaphoric relation between the body of material and its representative images. Freud found that the analysis of dreams is often complicated by the fact that the remembered images take the place of material that is repressed (the things we really don't want to recognize or remember). As I will subsequently develop these ideas in relation to black women's writing (in particular the chapters on Hurston, Morrison, and Marshall), condensation is what enables metaphorical images to capture history, which for its duration and multiplicity would otherwise require numerous volumes. Metaphor is also what gives expression to aspects of history that the writers themselves may not wholly recognize. The combination of condensation and metaphor defines black women's novels as both modernist and historical. This interpretation may appear to be at odds with the generally accepted notion that literary realism best reflects history. In fact, realism may well reflect history, whereas modernism, by way of condensation, embodies it. This is what makes the writing of black women so thought-provoking and so fraught with contradiction.

In a long article on William Faulkner's "The Bear," I documented how this story by an avowed conservative ideologue articulates the contradictions of race and class in its definition of the characters, their traits, and their relationships.[16] I would like, here, briefly to cite a counterexample from the other end of the political spectrum, Cuba's Nicolas Guillén—whose writing will give another perspective on the Afro-American tradition. I have always been struck by one of Guillén's early poems written before the Revolution and all the more powerful for its great expression of yearning for change. The poem is called, "Casa de la Vecindad" and in it Guillén describes Cuba as "Neighborhood house, patio to the Caribbean."[17] The line is crucial for our understanding of metaphor as the trope best able to embody contradiction. It is as if the phrase were saying two things at once. "Neighborhood house" suggests the squalor of a poorhouse and the familiarity of the barrio—a place where people might languish and die, or conversely, a setting for the warmth of rum and the cadence of a "son" guitar. Similarly, "patio to the Caribbean" also conveys both positive and negative associations: the inferiority of a back porch or stepping-stone to the real, more important world; and the pleasurable seclusion of Latin American architecture and life-style. In fact, Guillén's words are saying two things at once and this is precisely how they express larger historical contradictions. Cuba is perceived both as it is: the oppressed preserve of imperialism—and as it might be if one can imagine a postindependence Cuba that did not then come directly under the influence of United States capitalism.

But what Cuba is also includes its future. The contradictions of prerevolutionary Cuba will be the means of its transformation. Thus, the poem ends with images of blood and another set of twofold meanings, bound up and resolved as one:

> Here I am with my harsh-"son" guitar
> trying to bring out a song.

A song of frenzied dreaming,
a simple song of death and life
with which to greet the future drenched in blood,
red as the sheets, as the thighs,
as the bed
of a woman who's just given birth.[18]

The blood of birth that holds the possibility for death as well as
life is the poem's metaphor for its unspoken referent: revolution.
Only revolution negates the antithesis between life and death
that has haunted all the poem's images. What binds them up is
the notion of a future, the "trumpet blast of The First Judge-
ment."[19] Only revolution unites the struggle of all people: the
poet whose anguished travail equates that of a woman in labor.

I'd like to return now to black women's fiction to show how
Marshall uses metaphor as the trope of contradiction. I'll focus
on an episode from *Brown Girl, Brownstones* that depicts Selina
trapped in an excruciating interview with an aggressively patron-
izing white woman. Made to see herself for the first time
through the eyes of racist white society, Selina understands the
full meaning of alienation. The blackness she grew up in is suddenly, under the white woman's scrutiny, held up in front of her
like an object. Horrified, Selina bolts for the door and runs without stopping until she drops from exhaustion:

> The woman's face, voice, touch, fragrance, pursued her as
> she careened through the maze of traffic and blurred white
> faces, past spiraling buildings ablaze with light. Car horns
> bayed behind her, the city's tumid voice mocked her flight.
> She ran until a stitch pierced her side and her legs cramped.
> Clutching her leg she limped—like an animal broken by a
> long hunt—into the deep entranceway of a vacant store and
> collapsed in the cold shadows there. And like an animal she
> was conscious only of pain. Long shafts of pain struck true
> and quivered in each muscle, her lungs wrenched from
> their sockets with each breath, her heart battered the wall
> of her chest as if, understanding the truth, it rejected her
> and wanted to escape. (*BGB*, 200)

In similar fashion to Guillén, it is as if Marshall suddenly started to tell two stories at once: the harrowing flight of the fugitive slave, pursued by the lights, voices, and baying dogs of the bloodthirsty overseers, and Selina's panic-sticken flight from white bourgeois persecution. In fact, the metaphor allows Marshall to overlap two historical moments, demonstrating that the contradictions born with capitalism's agrarian mode continue to inform urban society. The metaphor also suggests that if Selina is to overcome alienation and recover her selfhood, she must confront history. Selina's recognition of slavery, her experience of the way it reduced black people to animals, and her union with her race's struggle for freedom are necessary for her self-definition. Only by seeing herself as racist white society sees her—as something sinful, ugly, dark, and fearsome like the night—can Selina transform the manacles of their prejudice into the positive attributes of self. Not to face the reality of blackness as it is perceived in a racist society is to live a lie.

Selina's confrontation with history brings our discussion full circle. The relationship of black women writers to history is enacted in the unfolding of their protagonists' lives. The novels discussed in this volume qualify as historical novels in the fullest sense of the term. Indeed, I know of no other body of writing that brings Lukács' definition of the historical novel to such profound realization. Focusing on the work of Walter Scott and Honoré de Balzac, Lukács demonstrated how these authors broke with the Romantic tradition in the definition of their novel's central characters and in their conceptualization of history as the movement of "popular" forces. Crucial to Lukács' definition of the historical novel is the notion that "world-historical figures" must be shown to arise out of the forces of history. "Scott lets his important figures grow out of the being of the age, he never explains the age from the position of its great representatives, as do the Romantic hero-worshippers."[20] The crux of Lukács' definition of the hero is "typicality;" and he was much impressed that Scott very often demonstrated typicality by "building his novels round a 'middling' merely correct and never heroic 'hero'."[21]

As we read Lukács' basic tenets today, we are apt to remark how limited he was by his cultural and educational formation in relation to nineteenth-century European history and by his choice of nineteenth-century bourgeois fiction. Nevertheless, his deep understanding of history as class struggle makes possible his radical shift away from elitist concerns and toward a properly Marxian perspective where the "popular" or underclass is revealed as the source of historical definition. Lukács opens the way for us to take his definition of the historical novel and history itself a few steps further and a few steps closer to American history. Although Lukács was much impressed with James Fenimore Cooper, his interest in American writing was restricted to the nineteenth century. If he had ventured into the twentieth and included black women writers like Zora Neale Hurston, then he would have had to rethink his notion of the "typical." Instead of the "middling" character Lukács identifies in the novels of Walter Scott, black women's fiction develops protagonists whose "typicality" (the quality that best allows them to understand and represent a particular era) is their marginality. Lukács found Scott's heroes interesting because they made history visible, but, by their "middling" nature, they really did not participate in history. Rather, the great struggles and contradictions waged around them while they stood on "neutral ground."[22] In contrast, none of the characters in the historical novels written by black women has the luxury of "neutral ground." Rather than casting the "extreme, opposing social forces"[23] in relief, they embody these forces. The story of Sula—Meridian—Selina is the story of contradiction met and made visible in the thoughts and actions of these women who are history and its future.

2. Wandering

Zora Neale Hurston's Search for Self and Method

> I used to climb to the top of one of the huge chinaberry trees which guarded our front gate, and look out over the world. The most interesting thing that I saw was the horizon. (*DT*, 36)

When, as a teenager, Zora Neale Hurston took a job as a lady's maid to a young starlet in a traveling Gilbert and Sullivan troupe, she became an instant success, a new "play-pretty" for the entire company. To explain the fascination the actors and musicians felt for her, Hurston discounts the fact that she was the only black in the group and attributes her popularity, instead, to her Southernness, particularly her use of language:

> I was a Southerner, and had the map of Dixie on my tongue. They were all Northerners except the orchestra leader, who came from Pensacola. It was not that my grammar was bad, it was the idioms. They did not know of the way an average Southern child, white or black, is raised on simile and invective. They know how to call names. It is an everyday affair to hear somebody called a mullet-headed, mule-eared, wall-eyed, hog-nosed, 'gator-faced, shad-mouthed, screw-necked, goat-bellied, puzzle-gutted, camel-backed, butt-sprung, battle-hammed, knock-kneed, razor-legged, box-ankled, shovel-footed, unmated so-and-so! Eyes looking like skint-ginny nuts, and mouth looking like a dishpan full of broke-up crockery! They can tell you in simile

26

exactly how you walk and smell. They can furnish a picture gallery of your ancestors, and a notion of what your children will be like. What ought to happen to you is full of images and flavor. Since that stratum of the Southern population is not given to book-reading, they take their comparisons right out of the barnyard and the woods. When they get through with you, you and your whole family look like an acre of totem-poles. (*DT*, 143–44)

Aside from the rich array of barnyard epithets, this passage includes another, more subtle feature, all the more suggestive of Hurston's relationship to language and writing. Contrary to the author's own good opinion of her grammar, the paragraph is based on a number of awkward and misleading shifts in the pronouns. This ungrammatical use of pronouns occurs throughout Hurston's autobiography, *Dust Tracks on a Road*, where it articulates the contradictory nature of Hurston's project as a black woman writer and intellectual attempting to mediate two deeply polarized worlds, whose terms include: South/North, black/white, rural/urban, folk tradition/intellectual scholarship. Hurston begins this passage with the first person and positions herself as a Southerner in opposition to the body of Northerners represented by the third-person pronoun "they." "*I* was a Southerner." "*They* were all Northerners." *They* did not know how a Southern child uses language. However, at this point, the third-person pronoun abruptly takes on a new referent. "*They* know how to call names." Here the pronoun represents Zora's own Southern neighbors, from whom Hurston now differentiates herself. She might have maintained her identification with the group of Southern speakers had she continued with the first person, using the pronoun "we" instead of shifting to the third person, "they."

The shift in pronouns is significant in relation to the introduction of the pronoun "you" later in the paragraph. "They can tell *you* in simile exactly how *you* look and smell" and so on. Who can this "you" be but the Northern audience, the white patron who financed much of Hurston's research and writing and the basically white, intellectual readership, who, in 1942, might have been expected to buy this book. The pronoun shifts have two functions. They suggest Hurston's inevitable turmoil and ambivalence over being in the middle and being mediator. And they suggest a certain smugness on the part of the author, "a poor black Southern girl" whose ungrammatical use of English is a deft ploy for turning the tables on the superior Northern establishment. One has the image of Hurston, standing back and chuckling over the "acre of totem-poles" she has just thrown in her reader's face, while she remains blameless because the shift in pronouns has separated the authorial "I" from the Southern "they."

Hurston's writing is full of tricks of this sort. As she explains in her introduction to *Mules and Men:*

> You see we are a polite people and we do not say to our questioner, "Get out of here!" We smile and tell him or her something that satisfies the white person because, knowing so little about us, he doesn't know what he is missing. The Indian resists curiosity by a stony silence. The Negro offers a feather-bed resistance. That is, we let the probe enter, but it never comes out. It gets smothered under a lot of laughter and pleasantries.[1]

Again the pronoun shifts enable Hurston to be both Southern and not-Southern, black and not-black, inferior and not-inferior. This is not to say that she assumes a Northern, white identity; rather, she lifts herself, as a writer, out of any possible inscription in the stigmatized view of Southern blackness. Bear in mind that this is the Jim Crow South. The passage is a remarkable example of how grammatical tricks make "feather-bed resistance" a form of subversion, whose deep hostility is masked by the displacement of aggression into "laughter and pleasantries." The entering "probe," and unmistakable image of invasion and male domination, is neatly smothered by a feminine, castrating image, the "feather-bed," notwithstanding all the polite double-talk.

Nowhere is Hurston's subversive intent and smug demeanor more evident than in the conclusion to *Mules and Men*. Here, she tells the story of Sis Cat, who, having let one rat get away while washing her face and hands, decides to eat a second rat straight off. When the rat objects, "Where's yo' manners at, Sis Cat? You gong to eat 'thout washing yo' face and hands?" (*MM*, 252) Sis Cat responds:

> "oh, Ah got plenty manners, . . . But ah eats mah dinner and washes mah face and uses mah manners afterwards." So she et right on 'im and washed her face and hands. (*MM*, 252)

Hurston's concluding one-liner is: "I'm sitting here like Sis Cat, washing my face and usin' my manners" (*MM*, 252). Having just served up the body of black Southern folktales to the Northern white readership, Hurston, gloating like the cat who's just devoured a rat, asks her reader, Now, who's swallowed who? In identifying herself with the aggressor, Hurston takes the subversive intent of her writing one step further than she was able to with her use of pronoun shifts. Rather than the displaced "I," lifted above the terrain of struggle between North and South, white and black, she is here the wily predator, using her "manners"—her writing—with confidence and satisfaction.

I'd like to return to the litany of barnyard names that began this essay and so astounded Hurston's traveling companions. From "puzzle-gutted" to "knock-kneed" and "unmated" this is the raw idiom, which Hurston inherits as a Southerner, particularly one born soon after the turn of the century and raised in a rural environment, and which she, as a writer, will have to transform. Full of assertive expressivity, this is basically still an oral idiom; and as such, it is limited both as a means of communication and as the basis for narrative. Notwithstanding their aggressive intent and vivid imagery, these words do not constitute a language for the audience to whom the book is intended. It is, instead a delightful object, a "play-pretty," like Zora Neale herself, who at this point is a fifteen-year-old pretending to be twenty, a flirtatious and talkative lady's maid, who doesn't yet see herself as a writer nor her discourse as the production of narrative.

One of the tasks Hurston will face as a writer is to develop a literary mode of discourse out of a folk tradition whose basic component is name-calling. The task is complicated by the fact that the tradition includes some qualities that an assertive and resourceful writer like Hurston would want to preserve in the course of developing a more properly literary style. When, in her autobiography, Hurston recalls her introduction to Big Sweet, we sense the dramatic strength that name-calling entails. And we get a glimpse of a woman who accomplishes in her outspoken use of the vernacular what Hurston will eventually achieve in writing:

> I heard somebody, a woman's voice "specifying" up this line of houses from where I lived and asked who it was.
> "Dat's Big Sweet" my landlady told me. "She got her foot up on somebody. Ain't she specifying?" ...She was giving her opponent lurid data and bringing him up to date on his ancestry, his looks, smell, gait, clothes, and his route through Hell in the hereafter....his pa was a double-humpted camel and his ma was a grass-gut cow, but even so, he tore her wide open in the act of getting born, and so on and so forth. He was a bitch's baby out of a buzzard egg. (*DT*, 194–95)

Although "specifying" may "signify" within the group of "four or five hundred people on the 'job' [who] are listening to Big Sweet's 'reading,'" it would not "signify" for an audience outside the rural South as anything more than stereotypically provincial. Big Sweet cannot directly speak her life to the reader, but her image as Hurston describes her, foot up on her opponent's porch, invective in her mouth, can embody something of her experience and gutsy spirit. "Specifying" may be the most self-affirming form of discourse, but it is bound up by its inscription within a specific group of language users. And it is circumscribed, held in check, by the larger system of domination that defines the South and women like Big Sweet as marginal and inferior. As another of Hurston's informants makes clear in his rendition of a folktale, "specifying" is something you do to a neighbor or a fellow camp worker. It's not something you pull on a straw boss or "Ole Massa." As his story goes:

> During slavery time two ole niggers wuz talkin' an' one said tuh de other one, "Ole Massa made me so mad yestiddy till Ah give 'im uh good cussin' out. Man, Ah called 'im everything wid uh handle on it. (MM, 83)

When the second man is later upbraided by the master he, too, decides to cuss Ole Massa out. But contrary to his friend's experience, "Ole Massa had 'im took down and whipped nearly tuh death" (MM, 83). When the poor man asks his companion why he wasn't punished for the cussing he gave the master, the friend responds:

> "Man, you didn't go cuss 'im tuh his face, didja?"
> "Sho Ah did. Ain't dat whut you tole me you done?"
> "Naw, Ah didn't say Ah cussed 'im tuh his face. You sho is crazy. Ah thought you had mo' sense than dat. When Ah cussed Ole Massa he wuz settin' on de front porch an' Ah wuz down at de big gate." (MM, 83)

If we remember the wily cat who swallowed the rat, then we might say that Hurston's project is analogous to cussing out the master. But because her medium is the narrative, rather than oral language, she can't take refuge down at the gate and do her cussing out in private. Instead, she must do her "specifying" in the form of a book Ole Massa can hold in his hands and read on his very own porch.

Whether or not we decide Hurston's writing achieves the sub-version of domination inherent in its bold intent depends largely on how the act of "specifying" is transformed in the process of creating a literary language. As the distance between opponents is foreshortened and finally condensed into the narrative space between writer and reader, barnyard simile becomes metaphor and a lot of the invective is redirected. In line with the relationship between condensed metaphoric images and the raw material of history that I suggested in chapter 1, I want to emphasize that the development of metaphor as a literary language is what differentiates Hurston's writing from that of her more realist contemporaries like Ann Petry and makes her the precursor of today's great modernist writers like Toni Morrison and Paule Marshall. However, because Hurston's work defines the incipient stages of black modernism (which also includes Jean Toomer's unique book, *Cane*), not all of her metaphors are the highly condensed, multireferential figures we have come to associate with Morrison's writing. In fact, many of Hurston's images occupy a midway point between "specifying" and metaphor. These, although drawn from colloquial expression, represent a more complex form of describing than the simple "calling out" and naming. One such example occurs as Hurston continues her account of Big Sweet. Recognizing the importance of befriending Big Sweet, Hurston remarks on her own feeling of insecurity and estrangement in the Polk County mill camp. As she puts it, "I felt as timid as an egg without a shell" (*DT*, 196). And no wonder—with men and women carrying knives and apt to do more than "specify" at each other, Hurston was definitely in a precarious position. Describing herself as a "bootlegger," she showed an inordinate interest in the camp's male population—their songs, stories, and general practice of "woofing" on each other. Big Sweet would prove herself an important ally and life-saver. In her own advice to Hurston, "You just keep on writing down them lies. I'll take care of all the fighting. Dat'll make it more better, since we done made friends" (*DT*, 197).

When Hurston describes herself as feeling "as timid as an egg without a shell," she evokes absolute vulnerability and she does so in a language that is only one step removed from the barnyard, but on its way to a frame of reference that will no longer be purely animal. "Specifying" equates the opponent with a brute, and, by the very nature of animal existence, cannot give symbolic expression to feelings. In contrast, the colloquial image, even though it is still rooted in a rural system of specification, gives ample space for the expression of emotion. This is possible not only because of the explicit comparison "as timid as," but because the shell-less egg is no longer strictly a part of nature in the same way as a "puzzle-gutted" and "knock-kneed" animal is.

The "egg without a shell" is also a particularly female image. This is true because the egg is the most basic female cell and because eggs—especially shell-less ones, in pans and ready to be fried—summon up the range of women's domestic labor. Hurston often draws from this same register in the creation of images based on colloquial expressions. A good example occurs in her most widely read novel, *Their Eyes Were Watching God*. Janie's grandmother has just finished describing her own life in slavery, the care she lavished on her daughter, who, nevertheless, went astray, abandoning her baby daughter, Janie, into the grandmother's care. In giving this account of her trials and tribulations, the grandmother is attempting to justify the marriage she has arranged between her young granddaughter and a middle-aged, pinch-penny farmer, Logan Killicks. Janie, who dreams of love and self-fulfillment, objects to the arranged marriage, knowing full well that although Killicks might never beat her, he'd sure plan on working her like a mule. But Janie's grandmother wins out. Appealing to Janie to consider her tired bones and old age as well as the hardships she has endured to secure Janie's future, the grandmother pleads, "Have some sympathy fur me. Put me down easy, Janie, Ah'm a cracked plate."[2]

With this expression, the grandmother confronts Janie with

all the accumulated years of her domestic toil—both in her own home and in the kitchen of her white employer. She demands that Janie experience guilt for her grandmother's unfulfilled life and recognize her responsibility to care for her grandmother by respecting her decisions. The image evokes self-pity and domestic blackmail—perhaps the two most oppressive aspects of any mother-daughter relationship in this culture. It will be some twenty years before Janie finally comes to realize the awful burden her grandmother placed in her hands the day she called herself a "cracked plate."

What enables Hurston to transcend colloquialisms such as these and write more complex and condensed metaphors is the same element of distance that allows her to look back on and study the folklore she was born into. As she puts it:

> From the earliest rocking of my cradle, I had known about the capers Brer Rabbit is apt to cut and what the Squinch Owl says from the house top. But it was fitting me like a tight chemise. I couldn't see it for wearing it. It was only when I was off in college, away from my native surroundings, that I could see myself like somebody else and stand off and look at my garment. (*MM*, 8)

When Hurston remarks that her culture once fit "like a tight chemise," she describes a situation most women will recognize as their own. Women wear their daily lives like a snug and intimate article of clothing, so familiar it's apt to be taken for granted. Very often only a significant transformation in situation or consciousness will bring women to scrutinize their daily surroundings and relationships. Another great writer of the Southern experience, for instance, is Harriette Arnow, whose documentation of rural Appalachian history and culture equals Hurston's collection of folklore and hoodoo medicine. Arnow (in her novel *The Dollmaker*,[3] first published in 1954) gives an even fuller account than Hurston's autobiography of the sort of changes women must experience in order to see themselves and

their culture in critical perspective. For Hurston, the move
North, the urban environment, the Barnard education created
the distance between herself and the once-tight chemise. For
Arnow, migration North included proletarianization and an introduction to mass culture. And for both women, the gift of radical hindsight is paid for by estrangement. Hurston's simple
expression of alienation, "I could see myself like somebody
else," can be read in two ways. Either she could see herself as if
she had become somebody else, or as if she were miraculously
split in two, her old self standing there with her new self looking
on. In any case, there is a sense of schizophrenia, not only between the self and the cultural garment, but deep within the self
as well.

Distance and alienation, then, give rise to some of the most
beautiful images set forth in the history of black women's writing. Looking back on her childhood, but seeing it from her perspective as an adult, Hurston describes a memorable dream
image:

> for weeks I saw myself sitting astride of a fine horse. My
> shoes had sky-blue bottoms to them, and I was riding off to
> look at the bellyband of the world. (*DT*, 45–46)

This delightful image is Hurston's response to a friend's refusal
to join her in a quest for the horizon. Always a wanderer, she re-
counts many instances of stifled wanderlust in her autobiography. Throughout her childhood, the desire for mobility would
very often work its way out in images such as these until the day
when, as a teenager, she would make her own "dust tracks on a
road" headed North. The image of shoes with "sky-blue bot-
toms" captures the clarity and mind-stretching creativity of the
best surrealist art. It elides a child's vocabulary and boundless
desire with a sophisticated notion of the world turned topsy-
turvy. With the sky brought down to earth and made accessible,
one might easily capture the world's "belly-band."

Not all of Hurston's meditations on journey are couched in

such positive terms. Very often the desire to wander is described as a compulsion that began in earnest with her mother's death:

> That hour began my wanderings. Not so much in geography, but in time. Then not so much in time as in spirit. (*DT*, 97)

As we so often find in Paule Marshall's writing, journey for Hurston is a quest for self. But as Hurston makes clear, although the self at the end of the road may be articulate, speaking and writing will have been bought at the price of the individual's alienation.

Echoing throughout Hurston's phrases about wandering and writing, both in her autobiography and elsewhere, is the strong influence of time and place. In many ways, the claim for time and place is at odds with the evolution toward alienation. In order to tell her story, Hurston cautions the reader, "you will have to know something about the time and place where I came from" (*DT*, 11). She goes on to demonstrate that time and place are more than contextual backdrop:

> Like the dead-seeming, cold rocks, I have memories within that came out of the material that went to make me. Time and place have had their say. (*DT*, 11)

This is another seemingly simple statement whose subtle complexities reside in metaphoric allusion. Essentially, Hurston is saying that her becoming a writer is tantamount to a rock learning to talk. In fact, the rocks will talk through her. And who are these "dead-seeming, cold rocks" but the tens of thousands of rural black women, considered less than beasts and denied a voice in history and letters.

In writing, Hurston stakes a claim to time and place for her own sake and for the sake of all the women and men whose stories will not reach our eyes and ears. Her efforts have far-reaching implications. For, in claiming a right to time and place, she contests the essential nature of capitalist society, which inscribes time and place within property relationships. Those who own property and control the means of production control time and place as well (both in the home and the workplace). When black women write to reclaim time and place, they do so outside of property relationships. This is true of Hurston, whose folktales fill the interstices of her informants' workdays and whose tale-telling takes place in those areas, like the jooks and the front porches, that are not included in either the system of industrial production or domestic labor. Tale-telling, like tale gathering, is something you do on the "job" when there is no job.

In her conception of time and place as self-defining and affirming and in her recovery of temporal and spatial zones outside of property relationships, Hurston lays the basis for Toni Morrison's conceptualization of Pilate in *Song of Solomon*. Pilate is another wanderer whose journey from the mountains of Virginia to Detroit is as much a journey through the geography of spirit as it is through concrete time and space. Pilate makes a point of telling people of her abiding interest in geography as if it were a personal attribute like texture of hair and shape of nose. Pilate, who has no possessions in the capitalist sense, has gathered and saved a rock from every place she has visited; just as Hurston, decades earlier, gathered and preserved folktales from the "dead-seeming, cold rocks" she met in sharecropping villages and turpentine camps. The geography that constitutes Pilate's spirit and the rhythm of her domestic space are, finally, the direct antitheses of her brother's propertied conception of space and time. For Macon Dead, the slumlord, rents are the equivalent of his tenants' spatial allotments in relation to their earning power.

Whereas Morrison's portrayal of Pilate offers an alternative to capitalist society, a household devoted to nonaccumulation, Hurston's claim to time and place fails to project a wholly new and positive reworking of social relationships. Most often, Hurston remains locked into the motif of wandering, trapped in a geography of spirit that is independent of property relationships and domination, but unable to transform the metaphoric geography into an alternative notion of daily life. The image of Hurston, in her dusty Chevy, bouncing over the Florida back roads from camp to camp, translates the spirit of wanderlust but doesn't prefigure an alternative form of society (as will be the case years later in Morrison's depiction of Pilate).

Hurston's lack of an alternative vision informs much of her writing about herself with desolation:

> I had always thought I would be in some lone, arctic waste land with no one under the sound of my voice. I found the cold, the desolate solitude, and earless silences, but I discovered that all that geography was within me. It only needed time to reveal it. (*DT,* 123)

Clearly, the cold and solitude have very little to do with the fear of being exiled to an "arctic wasteland." What Hurston is really worried about is not having anyone "under the sound of [her] voice." Her fear as a teller of tales is the "earless silence." The image captures the dread felt by an untried black woman, who would be a writer, of casting her words into a void. This is a fear which has long haunted black peoples' writing in this hemisphere. It goes back into the time of slavery, when many slaves who placed their narratives in the hands of abolitionists sensed that they were casting their words on a sea of uncertainty like messages in a bottle.[4] Although times had changed and so had the publishing industry, Hurston could well appreciate the anxiety of the slave narrator over getting a book published, keeping it in print, and having it well distributed. When she summons up an "arctic wasteland," then tells us "that all that geography was within [her]," we are made to realize in very concrete terms the burden of her uncertainty, to trace as we read the topography of her doubt as she expresses herself in image and metaphor.

However, the process of writing also involves the choice and development of the larger form of the narrative. As I see it, Hurston defined and worked in two very different forms, both of which express a social form as well as an aesthetic model. The first of these is exemplified by the collection *Mules and Men*, whose narrative topography includes the self-contained islands of the tales themselves, which are then interconnected and defined on a broader grid by the path of Hurston's journey and her conversations with the tale-tellers. The oral tales are the original text, which Hurston contextualizes through her own discourse and work as an anthropologist, finally producing yet another, properly literary, text: the book *Mules and Men*. The most basic formal feature to arise out of these layers of textualization is containment. This is a codifying and concretizing form that allows no room for narrative transformation. It is a text whose form mimetically reproduces the economy and social structures of the rural South. The tales, like the work camps, include great creative and human energies, but both are contained: the tale, by the closure of its form; the camps, by their isolation one from another and by their inscription within a larger economic system of domination. Although the camps were in many ways privileged zones, where men and women could hide from the long arm of white, Southern justice, these zones were included in a larger system, which required cheap labor, and so defined a part of its work force as "criminals."

How, then, does the figure of Hurston relate to the form of narrative containment? Born and raised only miles away from the Polk County work camps, she has returned as an anthropologist trained by Franz Boas and funded by a wealthy patron. As a mediator, her task is to transform the raw material of culture into a form accessible to a Northern, intellectual clientele. As a figure in the narrative, Hurston establishes and articulates links between the closed units represented by the tales. Her discourse creates the web of narrative context while it separates the tales from the bed of social context. Hurston's mobility and the larger text she writes break down the sense of closure that defines each tale told in isolation, but she does not so transform the tales as to make of them some new narrative form.

Part of the reason why the folktales themselves resist transformation resides in their internal structure, which, like the whole of Hurston's text, reflects the economics of an oppressed area as it is contained within a larger capitalist economy. A close reading of a single tale will demonstrate how these narratives partake of economic structures.

The story, which tells of Jack and the Devil, is typical of all the Devil stories in *Mules and Men* even though it is longer than most tales and includes more detail and narrative transitions. It is important to note that the Devil, although he has power and represents authority, is in no way comparable to the Ole Massa. The Devil, a trickster like the Jack or John of the stories, is an alternative representation of the black man, who, because he is an otherworldly figure, is not completely inscribed within the economic and social restraints common to the black population.

The story opens with an inheritance distributed equally between two brothers. The first brother uses his share to buy "a big farm" and "a pair of mules" (*MM*, 52), and to settle down. This is the last we hear of this brother. What follows is all about the second brother, Jack, who "took his money and went on down the road skinnin' and winnin' " (*MM*, 51).

Why is the first brother even mentioned? His part is very small and he's of no interest. Nevertheless, his function in the story is absolutely crucial. For the first brother represents the larger economy, the system of stability based on property ownership within which Jack's "skinnin' and winnin' " is inscribed. Although the whole of the story will focus on Jack's inventive and alternative economics, everything Jack does is contained by the system of capital that is in no way influenced or affected by the forms of exchange employed by Jack.

The first of these modes of exchange is gambling and features Jack pitted against an unbeatable opponent, who, having won all of Jack's money, suggests they keep the game going by staking Jack's life against "all de money on de table" (*MM*, 52). This is a good lesson in the forms of equivalence that evolved under capitalism, which equates a human being with currency. The attachment of exchange value to human beings is, of course, as old as slavery, capitalism's first mode of labor control in this hemisphere.

Jack agrees to the wager, loses, and suddenly finds himself facing a "twelve-foot tall" opponent. "De man looked down on 'im and tole 'im says, 'De Devil is mah name and Ah live across de deep blue sea' " (MM, 52). Within the terms of the wager and certainly by reason of his greater power, the Devil could kill Jack on the spot. But that would make a dull story and an unprofitable economics. As the Devil will show, and in keeping with the economics of slavery, Jack is more valuable alive than dead. So the Devil perpetuates the game, but changes its form, and in so doing, lifts Jack out of the economics of slavery and reconstitutes his relationship to him in terms of a system defined by debt peonage, not unlike the sharecropping system of the post–Civil War South.

The transformation to this new economic mode occurs after a transitional interlude in the story during which Jack must journey across the ocean to the Devil's house "befo' the sun sets and rise again" (MM, 52). Jack accomplishes the journey on the back of a bald eagle, whom he must feed in midflight "everytime she holler." He has brought along a yearling bull for the eagle's meals. The first time the eagle hollers, "Jack was so skeered dat instead of givin' de eagle uh quarter of de meat, he give her de whole bull" (MM, 53). This puts Jack in a terrible fix when the eagle makes a subsequent demand for food. Jack's response is to tear off his own arm and then a leg, so that when he finally arrives at the Devil's house and knocks on the door, he identifies himself as, "One of de Devil's friends. One widout uh arm and widout uh leg" (MM, 54). The Devil quickly remedies the situation because, as we shall see, he wants an able-bodied worker, not a cripple:

> Devil tole his wife, says: "Look behind de do' and hand dat man uh arm and leg." She give Jack de arm and leg and Jack put 'em on. (MM, 54)

What's remarkable about this passage is not Jack's self-mutilation and acquisition of new limbs per se. Such things happen throughout the mythic stories of Africa, the roots of the Afro-American storytelling tradition, as in Amos Tutuola's *The Palm-Wine Drinkard*,[5] which at one point describes a man who, journeying from the market to his own village, returns all the limbs and body parts he borrowed from other people on his way to town. When he finally arrives home he is only a head. The Afro-American folktale, as Hurston records it, regards the loss and acquisition of body parts with the same matter-of-fact attitude we find in Tutuola's mythic writing. These narratives shift the focus away from the notion of a body as it belongs to an individual who might experience pain and loss; they demand that we instead consider the process of transformation itself and what it implies. Broadly speaking, the incident articulates the fluctuations in fortune an individual might experience. Gambling, sharecropping, and all the conniving schemes anyone like Jack might invent hold out the promise of instantaneous reward and the probability of rapid downfall. One minute, you're on top of the world; the next, you're hobbling around barely able to survive; and then, you're miraculously restored. The story of the eagle is a mythic device for describing the worldview of people whose lives ultimately are in someone else's hands.

Once at the Devil's house, Jack quickly learns his new economic status. Now in the Devil's debt for his arms, legs, and life, Jack is required to perform a number of tasks. With his labor, given in exchange for a debt that can never be paid, Jack now symbolizes another era in the economic history of this hemisphere, an era that assigned the Indians of Latin America to the haciendas and the emancipated blacks of North America to the peonage of sharecropping. First, Jack must clear a hundred acres for the Devil; then he must retrieve a lost ring from the bottom of a well; and finally, he must pluck two geese in a raging gale without losing a single feather. Luckily, Jack, who could never

have performed the tasks in the amount of time allotted by the
Devil, is aided by the Devil's daughter, who magically completes
each of the tasks. It should be noted the women figures in the
tales are never portrayed as stereotypically subservient peasant
women, but exercise free will, guile, and intelligence. They
make their own decisions and form their own alliances, often
contrary to the wishes of male figures in positions of
authority.[6]   The conclusion of the story features a new set of economic relationships. Jack, having fulfilled his obligations to
the Devil, marries his daughter and sets up housekeeping. The
situation suggests his liberation from bondage and access to a
form of freeholding. Although the Devil might be forced to accept Jack's independence as the logical result of their contract,
he, as a domineering master, fails to accept the situation emo-
tionally. This is evident one night when the Devil comes looking to kill Jack. As a free man, Jack is now worth more dead than
alive. This is the reverse of his economic definition under slavery. Hurriedly, Jack and his wife escape in a buckboard pulled by
two of the Devil's horses with the Devil in pursuit on his jump-
ing bull.

The outcome of this section of the story has to do, significantly, with the manipulation of language. It suggests the historical function of black language and writing from slavery to the
present, which has often reversed systems of domination. The
horses Jack has stolen are booby-trapped. Named "Hallowed-be-
thy-name" and "Thy-Kingdom-Come," they've been trained to
fall to their knees every time the Devil calls their names. Jack is
able to outdistance the Devil only because his wife knows the
charm to reverse the Devil's spell each time he calls out. However, the Devil finally catches up with Jack, who has hidden in a
hollow log, where he invents his own language trick to turn the
tables on the Devil. When the Devil picks up the log, Jack cries
out, "O Lawd, have mercy" (*MM*, 58). His speech act parallels
the Devil's use of holy names and has the effect of causing the

Devil such a fright that he drops the log and attempts to flee. But in his haste, he orders his bull to turn around with such ferocity that "De jumpin' bull turnt so fast till he fell and broke his own neck and throwed de Devil out on his head and kilt 'im" (*MM*, 58). So the Devil is mastered by himself and by Jack in the use of language.

"Dat's why dey say Jack beat de Devil" (*MM*, 58). The conclusion of the story is a statement of closure. It separates the tale from the workers' daily lives. Although the story's characters and their relationships have spoken for the real-life situations of black people in this country, these lessons do not carry over to the daily life and toil in the camps. The story is a unit whose function is not to transform anyone's thoughts about his or her working and living conditions. Rather, the story and its telling affirm the group as a cohesive unit, whose members' real-life possibilities are just as contained as the form of the stories they tell.

Group definition and affirmation are the positive features of these stories, whose form, like the society in which they occur, denies transformation. Affirmation is their strength, but it is a strength evolved in response to containment. A good example are the stories of one-upmanship. One man begins: "I know land so poor it won't grow rocks." Thereafter, each of the tellers must respond with another, more impoverished and humorous example. The formula is the same in the "I-know-a-man-blacker-than" stories and the "uglier-than" stories.

> "Ah seen a man so ugly till he could get behind a jimpson weed and hatch monkies.
> Everybody laughed and moved closer together. Then Officer Richardson said: "Ah seen a man so ugly till they had to spread a sheet over his head at night so sleep could slip up on him."
> They laughed some more, then Clifford Ulmer said:
> "Ah'm goin' to talk with my mouth wide open. Those men y'all been talkin' 'bout wasn't ugly at all. Those was

pretty men. Ah knowed one so ugly till you could throw him in the Mississippi river and skim ugly for six months." (*MM*, 73).

Who wins in a "lying" contest? Is it the best man and the best tale? Or is it the group, "Everybody laugh[ing] and mov[ing] closer together"? Telling stories like these affirms the group more than its individual members. It allows each participant to experience the force of cohesion. But it does so on the basis of derision, and this, too, is a feature of the oppressive system that contains the storytellers and their tales. The stories look at blackness like they look at ugliness. They affirm race, but they do not then transcend racial prejudice. This is, instead, the project for our time. The stories Hurston records begin in negativity; seize their negativity; and in so doing, position themselves on the brink of formulating an alternative vision. But they go no further. This is the significance of "lying," the rural black word for storytelling. From the point of view of the dominant white population, "Niggers lie and lie" (*DT*, 49). Seizing the negativity, the black folk tradition affirms the right to "lie"—to tell tales— to give shape to the self and community. But "lying" can go no further because so long as racial domination exists, "lying" cannot transcend the boundary of otherness and inferiority defined from above.[7]

At this point, I'd like to look at Hurston's most remarkable book—remarkable because its narrative form does transcend containment. This is the novel *Their Eyes Were Watching God.* What makes this text so different from Hurston's other, more conventional, novels and at the same time defines it as the precursor for many contemporary novels by black women is its dialectical form. This is the form Paule Marshall develops in *Praisesong for the Widow* and Alice Walker brings to fruition in *The Third Life of Grange Copeland.* I emphasize the importance of the dialectical narrative because this is what enables a vision of the future. As we saw, the rural black narrative tradition was also influenced by a sense of history as dialectical process. This is evident in the tale of Jack and the Devil where Jack's relationship to domination is traced through three distinct economic modes: slavery, debt peonage, and freeholding.[8] Similarly, *Their Eyes Were Watching God* works through three historically produced economic modes. The great difference between the novel and the folktale is the way we experience the novel, for the most part, as a universal process that is not contained or inscribed in some larger oppressive economic system. This is due to the fact that text and context are not separate as they were in Hurston's collection of folk tales. Rather than the sense of closure evoked at the end of each tale and enhanced by the difference between Hurston's mobility and the static isolation of the camps, the novel welds the authorial persona to the figure of the protagonist, Janie Woods, and articulates its dialectic through her movements through geography and through three very different relationships to men. The economics of marriage are, in this novel, the figuration for larger historical forms.

Janie's relationship to her first husband, Logan Killicks suggests the system of sharecropping. Although Killicks does not himself work on shares, he allows us to perceive how the society itself is locked into a system of debt peonage. Then, too, in what Killicks expects from his wife, he is really no different from the sharecroppers he has managed to rise above. Hurston shows a deft sense for the influence of the forces of history on people's lives in refusing to portray Killicks as a personally mean man. If he regards his young wife as a mule, it is because in this system of backbreaking rural labor, women were expected to bear the burdens of fieldwork as well as domestic toil. Killicks wants a woman who will plow alongside him, cut up "seed taters," move manure, and accept sex whenever and however he wants it. There is no room for frivolity and spontaneity. Spring is not a set of lacy leaf patterns, as Janie would like to see it, but a set of tasks to be performed. The brutality of this system is not necessarily related to physical violence and abuse. Killicks has never laid a hostile hand on Janie. Rather, it resides in the stifling of dreams; the death of spirit; the denial of art, imagination and creativity.

So when Joe Starks comes whistling down the road, "cityfied" and "stylish" (*EWW*, 47), Janie cannot help but see in him the possibility for her self-fulfillment. The problem is that Janie confuses manner and style with creativity and dreams. She doesn't realize that these indicators of success are merely signs for another, equally stifling economic mode. Janie runs off with Joe and the two of them make their way to Eatonville, Florida, an all-black town, which under Joe's leadership, will soon become a model for progress, as it has been defined by dominant, white urban society. Joe gives the town its post office, store, and street lamp, and presides over all in a most paternalistic way.[9]

Again Hurston avoids overpersonalizing the terms of Janie's relationship to Joe and allows us to see the economic factors that condition their life together. Joe Starks represents the nascient black bourgeoisie, hell-bent for progress and ready to beat white society at its own game. In the more cutthroat atmosphere of the urban North where property ownership and land speculating mediate race prejudice, Joe might have more closely resembled Toni Morrison's portrayal of Macon Dead. In the rural South and the racially calm atmosphere of Eatonville, Joe is at his ease to evolve a more provincial model of bourgeois domination. But it is nonetheless oppressive. Joe may glad-hand everybody, but he runs the town with a loud mouth, a big belly, and an iron will.

In this situation, the degree of Janie's oppression is no less than it was on the farm. Only the terms of the oppression have changed. As the wife of the town's leading citizen, Janie is denied self, voice, and sexuality. She must dress in a decorous fashion, taking particular care to tie up her hair, lest any other man share in the sensual pleasure reserved for her husband. She may wait on customers in the store; but she may not speak out of turn, and she may certainly not offer an opinion or join in any rowdy behavior like playing checkers or telling tales. If Janie was a beast of burden in her first life, she has, in her bourgeois life, become a domestic pet. Like Matt Bonner's starved and abused yellow mule, which her husband turns into the town mascot, Janie was freed from brutal labor and turned into an object. And if Logan Killicks rebuked her for her failure to do her share of the work, Joe Starks made Janie bear the weight of constant derision for the inadequacies and stupidity he daily brought to her attention.

In describing Janie's relationship to her third husband, Hurston offers a utopian betrayal of history's dialectic. She chooses not to depict the Northern migration of black people, which brought Hurston herself to New York and a college degree and brought thousands of other rural blacks to the metropolis and wage labor. In this, Hurston sets a precedent in black women's writing that will leave unexplored the possibility of a black working-class culture in this country. By their absence from her novel, industrialization, the city, the black working class are not shown to represent the future for black people.

Instead, Janie and Tea Cake evolve their relationship on the "muck," whose very name suggests something of a primal never-never land, more south than the rural South. Perhaps the "muck," or "glades" as it's sometimes called, articulates the recovery of Caribbean culture. Indeed, Janie learns to sing and dance with the Bahamians who also work on the "muck." Then, too, it summons up images of precapitalist societies: the Seminoles and renegade black slaves who allied with them. The "muck," as Hurston portrays it, is a mythic space with just enough reference to migrant agricultural workers to give it credibility.

We might criticize Hurston for situating the utopian future in an economic reality we know to be highly exploitative, but what's more important here is how the "muck"—and some atypical economic aspects Janie and Tea Cake bring to it—allow Hurston to develop a truly reciprocal relationship between Janie and her husband. This is possible because Janie and Tea Cake are really not inscribed within the economics of the "muck." If they plant and harvest beans, they do so because they enjoy fieldwork and because it allows them to live in the heart of Southern black cultural production. They are not, like many of the other migrant workers, bowed down by debts and kids. In fact, Janie and Tea Cake do not fit into any larger economic model. Janie, with a large inheritance in the bank, need not work at all and Tea Cake, whose forte is gambling, need never accept a job unless he wants it. Lifted out of economic constraints by their atypicality, Tea Cake and Janie are free to experience work as an enjoyable and fulfilling endeavor, whose capacity to give pleasure is only slightly less than sex, music, and a plate of baked beans.

Throughout Janie's three relationships, Hurston demonstrates how a woman's sexuality is defined in relation to the economics of heterosexuality in male-dominated situations. The instant Janie's grandmother catches her kissing a boy over the garden fence, she is defined as a functioning heterosexual woman. The grandmother's immediate decision to contract Janie's marriage clearly shows that a woman's role in this society is to be put into the circuit of male exchange. Janie's value is her virginity and possessability. As an object destined for male ownership, she can have no aspirations for selfhood. These girlish desires must be put on the shelf until her fiftieth birthday, when, if she has outlived her husband, she might once again sit under a springtime pear tree and contemplate what's left of the future.

In her relationship with Killicks, Janie's sexuality is subsumed under her ability to produce. The strength of her back in the field and her arm in the kitchen are worth more than her function in bed. From Killicks's point of view, Janie's sexuality is the place where he puts his penis. Since sex is intended to satisfy his need, rather than Janie's desire, it doesn't matter that he refuses to wash his dirty, stinking body before getting into bed with his wife. Killicks might grant Janie a biology, but he and the economics of rural impoverishment reduce women's sexuality to animal need, with the male animal on top.

With her second marriage, Janie's sexuality enters into a system of display and exchange defined by the market under capitalism. If she was little more than an animal for her first husband, she is essentially a commodity for her second. In this system, Janie's sexuality is lifted out of the economics of production and redefined by consumption. Thus, appearance takes precedence over strength. And this is the basis for the contradiction between male domination and patriarchy on the one hand and the capitalist market system on the other. Hurston clearly senses the contradiction in her depiction of the tension between Joe Starks' possessive domination of his wife and his desire that she be on display and available—but modestly, like the canned goods on his store's shelf. To say simply that such a system makes women into objects does not fully express the fearful double bind that women are forced to live, having to be unquestionably loyal to their husbands, while making themselves accessible to other men's gaze. The system is, however, not without its hazards for the patriarch, whose deepest fear, as Joe Starks knows, is impotence.

With her third marriage, Janie is lifted out of all previously defined economic modes and male domination as well. Since possession and objectification do not define the dynamic of their union, Tea Cake and Janie are free to devote their energy and attention to maintaining reciprocity. When, at their first meeting, Tea Cake teaches Janie to play checkers, he sets the terms of their relationship in which all endeavor will be defined as sport and shared equally. Heterosexuality is neither a basis for power nor a reason for submission, but a mode in which a man and a woman might equally participate. Although Tea Cake and Janie enjoy frequent sex, they also like good food, evenings with friends, and afternoons spent hunting. When sex is not essentialized, sensuality may be found in all aspects of daily life.

Many who read *Their Eyes Were Watching God* for the first time are struck by the fact that Janie's happy relationship with Tea Cake comes to such an abrupt and tragic end. We might even want to accuse Hurston of literary overkill in making Tea Cake the victim of a mad dog's attack, and then portraying Janie confronted by her enraged hydrophobic husband and forced to shoot him down like a stray dog. The only way to avoid turning this otherwise very modernist text into a cliché of naturalism is to read Tea Cake's death in a figural way. The fact that he turns on Janie in his last hour reiterates the death of Janie's previous husband, Joe Starks, who, with his last breath, heaps blame and recrimination on Janie. Although Tea Cake and Joe Starks are worlds apart and in no other way comparable in their treatment of Janie, Hurston is making it clear in her portrayal of their dying moments that women cannot hope to have themselves fully realized in their husbands.

When Janie shoots the maddened Tea Cake, she not only saves her own life, she also steps outside of the male-defined circuit of exchange her grandmother thrust her into with her first marriage. Janie's killing of Tea Cake is the book's strongest statement. In terms of heterosexuality, it provides a far more radical response to potential domination than the utopian fantasy of life on the "muck" suggests in relation to economic exploitation. It demonstrates that no matter if Tea Cake was a truly supportive husband, as long as relationships between men and women are embraced by a larger system in which men dominate, no woman can expect to attain selfhood in marriage. The radical nature of Janie's symbolic claim for her own time and space is apparent in the events immediately following Tea Cake's death. The legal system and public opinion that seek to brand Janie a criminal and the ordeal of the courtroom hearing testify to the forces in this society that view a heterosexual female outside the male circuit as aberrant and in need of punishment.

This, however, is not the book's final moment. Rather, the novel opens and concludes with a back-porch conversation between Janie, who has just returned to Eatonville after Tea Cake's death, and her close friend, Pheoby Watson. Janie, her road-sore feet in a pan of water, a bowl of Pheoby's beans in her stomach, tells her story to her friend. The nucleus of their warm companionship counterbalances the recrimination of Tea Cake's friends who rose up against Janie when they first heard of the shooting, and it offers an alternative to the gossipy chatter of the townspeople who greet Janie's return with hostility born of narrow-mindedness. These are the images of the backward, oppressed, exclusionary community: women held back by men and men acting out of rivalry. In contrast, the image of Janie and Pheoby captures the spirit and hope for some new community based on sisterhood. This is not to suggest that in killing Tea Cake Janie has put an end to her heterosexuality. Rather, Janie has learned that although women must be with men and for men, they must also be with women and for women. Pheoby brings to the sisterhood her care of Janie's fatigued body; Janie supplies the lessons she has learned. Pheoby's exclamation is a vision of the future upon which the book closes:

> "Lawd!...Ah done growed ten feet higher jus' listenin' tuh you, Janie. Ah ain't satisfied wid mahself no mo'. Ah means tuh make Sam take me fishing wid him after this." (*EWW,* 284)

This is the book's most radical single statement.

3. Describing Arcs of Recovery

Paule Marshall's Relationship to Afro-American Culture

When at the end of *Brown Girl, Brownstones*, Selina Boyce removes one of her silver bracelets and tosses it high into the air, she performs a highly symbolic act that articulates not only her position as a young black woman, the daughter of Barbadian immigrants, ready to embark on her future. It also describes Paule Marshall's position as a writer, who as a young black woman and immigrant closely resembles her fictional character. Selina's bracelet is one of two she, like all Barbadian girls in the New York community, has worn since birth. The bracelet is a sign, reminding her of her folk heritage. One bracelet thrown, one bracelet kept—these two silver bands testify to Marshall's role as a writer, whose task has been to articulate the difficulties of being in two worlds at once and the need to unite the Afro-American cultures of North America and the Caribbean.

One bracelet thrown, one bracelet kept—Selina, Marshall's figural self, bids good-bye to her childhood and the Chauncey Street tenements and brownstones where she grew up. The bracelet, whose arc she traces across the moonlit sky and whose sharp clash marks its fall, gives testament to Selina as she has been formed by her community; it also represents her gift to those who will remain behind. The bracelet Selina keeps is her visible link to her Caribbean heritage; it also gives reference to all the lessons Selina has learned in the process of growing up and away. The delight of coming into adult sexuality, the heart-

break of couple relationships as they are defined under capitalism by property, the brutally demeaning nature of racism—these are the lessons Selina will take wherever she goes. In creating Selina as a figural representation of herself and her life struggles, Marshall lifts her character out of the individual and particular of the purely autobiographic mode and achieves through symbolic representation a means of expressing both the deep sensitivity of individual experience and the concerns of a much larger community. As we shall see, Marshall's great talent as a writer is her insightful portrayal of individual characters as they articulate the complex of a community's actions and desires. One bracelet thrown, one bracelet kept—this figural act also embodies Marshall's development as a writer, growing with each book and leaving a little something behind for us—her community of readers—these documents of experience that are her three novels.

The path traced by Selina's bracelet as it flies through space defines an arc on which we may plot Marshall's three novels as these constitute generationally defined points in a woman's life. Here, too, the individual expands into the historical as each of the three periods comes to suggest a different politically defined mode. *Brown Girl, Brownstones* is Marshall's novel about childhood. In focusing on the process of Selina's growing up, the novel moves from a bony and boisterous little girl to a supple and courageous young woman. Her childhood defined by partial knowledge, Selina attains womanhood having challenged the adult world and arrived at a deep understanding of her parents and the forces that have shaped their community. This novel's notion of history might also be characterized as youthful. At the novel's conclusion, with everything possible and nothing predictable, Selina prepares to step into the future. This view into history captures the spirit of the sixties, the Civil Rights Movement, racial awareness, and cultural revolution. Like Selina, history stands on the brink of unforeseen transformations, exuberant with potential but unable to grasp its specific nature.

Published ten years later, in 1969, *The Chosen Place, The Timeless People* is Marshall's novel of middle age. Merle, the protagonist, a woman in her forties, embodies the burdens of racial and social problems born with colonialism and the slave trade and reshuffled—but not solved—during the radical politics of the sixties. Her body no longer supple, a little loose flesh here and there, Merle represents a historical mode that has come to recognize its limitations and chooses to tackle only immediate, practical problems. This is a vision of history no longer capable of utopian imagination, but determinedly focused on a grim and contradictory reality. The transformation of history seems no longer to be possible, but the novel sees very little hope for changing history through reform. Its critical scrutiny of development projects in the Third World leaves the reader with a bankrupt sense of the future.

In contrast, Marshall's most recent novel, *Praisesong for the Widow*, captures again some of the enthusiasm generated by her first novel and suggests, if not the utopian aspirations of the sixties, then a visionary sense of renewal through the recovery of culture. It remains to be seen whether this will be an effective political strategy for the eighties. One certainty is that Marshall's notion of culture (and the people who produce culture) bears very little resemblance to the countercultural activities of the sixties, which were largely based in a youthful population. Instead, *Praisesong* is Marshall's novel of maturity, whose sixty-four-year-old protagonist, Avey Johnson, blends life's sobering lessons with the rediscovery of the child's aspirations. Her body encased in a long-line girdle, her spirit entombed in middle-class aspirations, Avey, by undergoing a process of liberation, rediscovers self, race, and community. Here, history is defined by a curious combination of transformation through cultural practice, which is then welded to a very American notion of what constitutes a utopian society, based, as we shall see, on the return to the rural small town.

So Marshall's writing does not span the generations in order finally to come full circle, but streaks off on her arcs of recovery always into the future whose specific content cannot be known except by suggestion at the end of each of the novels, or by reverse implication as a more recent novel sheds light on a previous one.

In tracing her arcs of recovery, Marshall implicitly raises the question of the urban environment and specifically whether American cities have proved to be fertile ground for the aspirations of black people. I think we might take Paule Marshall's writing as an example of how contemporary black women writers define themselves against the urban while at the same time recognizing the significant contribution city culture (and specifically the Afro-American culture born in the cities) made to their development. In writing *Praisesong*, Marshall dedicates her book to her grandmother and chooses for her epigraph a line from Amiri Baraka, reminiscing about his mother.[1] Taking these as clues to the novel's motivation, we sense that Marshall's primary endeavor is to retrieve the culture that shaped her mother's generation. This was the blues of the twenties and thirties, decades whose young people would be the adults of the forties. This was also a period deeply influenced by the Harlem Renaissance and the great vision of the city, so often depicted in Langston Hughes's poetry, as the new heart of the American black community. This is a poetry, which recognized the poverty and inequality of black people in comparison to the white world, yet nevertheless captured the great energy and strong hope the city held for black people newly emerging from rural poverty. Very little of this is present in Marshall's portrayal of the city. Except for brief moments when Selina gazes into a Fulton Street barroom and recognizes there in the talk, the songs, and the music the great vitality of black urban life, the city is cast as the means for integrating black people into a grinding labor mill out of which a few will emerge as the upwardly mobile black bourgeoisie, destined for the stifling life of the suburbs.

Nevertheless, the culture that defined city life is one of the things Marshall's writing works to retrieve. The other is the rich folk heritage of black people whose roots lie in rural peasant society. As someone whose own history includes the land-based economy of Barbados and the New York immigrant community, Marshall is well placed to articulate the twofold stream of cultural influence that has shaped all Afro-American people. It is clear in her writing that the importance of the rural comes to predominate over the urban as she constructs images of the future. The reason why this is so has much to do with the fact that she focuses on a segment of the American black population, which, by access to the professions, arrived at the wasteland of the suburbs. The city is thus equated with the breakdown of culture and not seen as the site for cultural renewal. Marshall's overall project as a writer is to salvage those cultural components generated by urban life that vitally shaped her mother's generation, and then weld these to the folk tradition. The wellspring of the future is, then, folk society—but a very particular folk society, which, like Avey Johnson, bears the scars inflicted by urban life.

Because the return to the folk tradition is primary, the most important arc traced in Marshall's writing is through geographic space from New York City and the years of her formation to the Caribbean, the land of her birth. Although this arc plots the recovery of black history in the New World and Afro-American culture, it does not exclude the personal or generational histories of Marshall's characters. Actually, Marshall's arcs are multidimensional and simultaneously include the individual and particular as well as the historic and communal.

If there is one thing that predominates in contemporary writing by black American women, it is the journey (both real and figural) back to the historical source of the black American community. For contemporary writers, the journey back probably originates with Hurston's flight from the city back to the South to drive the back roads, spend time in the small towns and sawmill camps, and collect the material that comprises her landmark text of Afro-American folklore, *Mules and Men*. By comparison to the black American literary tradition by male writers from Richard Wright to Ralph Ellison, Hurston represents an alternative tradition—one schooled in anthropology and devoted to the recovery of the source of Afro-American cultural life. Because culture is inextricably linked to the family and the community, it necessarily informs the nurturing roles performed by women. If there is something of a motherline running from the work of Hurston to that of contemporary black women writers, it is constituted largely on women's intimate knowledge of how nurturing is performed in culture and their deep interest in strengthening cultural identity.

Contemporary versions of the journey back include Paule Marshall's *Praisesong for the Widow* and Toni Morrison's *Song of Solomon*, which should be read as companion texts. Morrison's version sets its protagonist, Milkman, on an arduous journey away from the Northern industrial city of his birth, back to his family's origin in the rural South, and finally, on wings of myth, to the spiritual homeland in Africa. Milkman's overland trek becomes a metaphor for the recovery of racial and cultural identity as all the trappings of his Detroit city life and bourgeois class background are stripped from him—his watch, his expensive shoes, his shirt all fall by the wayside. Morrison uses something of the same paradigm—but in a more abstract form—in her most recent book, *Tar Baby*, whose journey of recovery terminates in the Caribbean, as it does in Marshall's writing. In *Tar Baby*, as in these other texts, the Caribbean is finally not the journey's end so much as its imaginative point of departure for the spiritual recovery of maroon and voodoo culture.

The difference between Morrison's journeys of return and those described by Marshall is the more personal nature of Marshall's writing. The characters in Morrison's recent novels—and this is the fate of both Milkman and Jadine, the "Tar Baby"—tend to lose the possibility of evoking the individual's experience and sensitivity for the sake of expressing a larger racial and

class typology. Thus, Milkman represents the Northern black
boy, born into an upwardly mobile family and destined to become a black professional. On the other hand, Jadine, an even
deeper abstraction, represents a jet-setter in black, a rootless
debutante artist and careerist. The abstract nature of *Tar Baby* is
even more apparent when we consider the fragmentary nature of
this novel's journey of return. Rather than presenting a single
character whose trajectory accomplishes the retrieval of culture,
Tar Baby brings together a random assortment of individuals
whose separate lives represent partial arcs of recovery. This includes the "tar baby" and the renegade she befriends, the black
servants and their white employers—all of whom combine to
suggest a failed version of the vision of social totality that concludes *Song of Solomon*.

By comparison, Marshall's Avey Johnson from *Praisesong* escapes the abstraction that informs Morrison's Milkman and "Tar
Baby." Yet Avey, for all her personable qualities and identifiably
individual character traits, still comes to embrace populations
larger than herself—the older black woman, the black mother,
the now-middle-class suburbanite black woman. This is Marshall's genius—to portray individual characters in such a way
that they suggest universals without losing the deeply human
qualities that make them memorable as individuals. She achieves
this by choosing to write about characters whose lives strike a
common chord with that of many black people in this country.
Her Avey Johnson, who has worked all her life and raised children, speaks to the great majority of black women, whereas
Morrison's Jadine, hopping from Paris to the Caribbean, speaks
only to their fantasies. Then, by situating her Avey Johnson, not
in the family and in the home, but on a journey from which she
looks back on family and home, Marshall lifts her character out
of a purely personal experience and makes her life's story our
means of access to the history of black people in the New World.
Finally, by employing female protagonists, Marshall's characters
are better able to yield up personal experience. Morrison's choice

of a male protagonist in *Song of Solomon* is an interesting experiment but in the end, Milkman's quest for self tends to reinvent the notion of patrimony that emerges even as he puts together his genealogy.

One thing Marshall definitely shares with Morrison is the understanding that the journey of recovery is long, arduous, and usually painful. In *The Chosen Place, The Timeless People*, the journey of retrieval is inscribed in the trajectory of Merle's migration from the Caribbean to London, back to the Caribbean, and finally on to Africa. But the notion of journey—and a long, sometimes tiresome one, at that—also penetrates the narrative, where we, as readers, experience its duration with each of the book's five-hundred pages. I once remarked to a friend (Hazel Carby), who teaches black women's fiction at Wesleyan University, that I couldn't understand why Paule Marshall, who had such a condensed—metaphoric—style in *Brown Girl, Brownstones*, should then employ such a traditional form of narrative in *The Chosen Place*—one whose interest is to detail every inch of topography (human and natural) that comprises the Caribbean island setting of the novel. My friend replied that the tedium is a necessary part of the author's journey to reclaim her Caribbean identity. And I'd say that it is a necessary part of the reader's journey, as well. We are meant to live the cyclical time of village life, meant to feel every bump and turn on the route from Bournehills to the capital (just as the peasants who will later labor to transport their sugar cane to the mill), meant also to experience the boring high-society parties given by the white colonial aristocracy, meant to have to work through the system of funding and support that constitute the development projects in the Third World, meant, finally, to experience all this as a duration—a journey of discovery and recovery. If we take Marshall's first and last books as literary epiphanies—novels whose conclusions signal the optimistic opening out into the future— *The Chosen Place* then represents the durational arc of journey. Its conclusion—the development project in a shambles and

Merle's longed-for reunion with her daughter in Africa an ambiguous future at best—describes, not a new and optimistic vision of the future, but the practicalities of the present.

If the journey of recovery in *The Chosen Place* is painstaking, it is deeply and humiliatingly painful in *Praisesong for the Widow*. Every shred of remembered experience Avey wrests from her past is won at great expense, both physical and emotional. When, during a dream, Avey is confronted by her now-dead husband, she experiences once more his recriminating gaze, and with it remembers the moments in their life together when she felt the erosion of her identity and their regard for each other. The dream brings Avey to realize that their journey up the social ladder coincided with their having lost or forsaken the Afro-American cultural heritage that had once filled their life with music and dance. Then, in another dream, Avey encounters her long-dead great-aunt Cuney, who, with beckoning gestures, urges Avey to follow her and in so doing recognize and reconstitute her link with slavery and the African nations. But Avey—no longer the seven-year-old who once followed her great-aunt on treks across Tatem Island—but a grandmother now, comfortably ensconced on a Caribbean cruise ship, refuses and lashes out at her aunt, the two of them struggling in Avey's dream, trading blow for blow until Avey awakens to find her body sore and bruised.

But recrimination, blows, and bruises are not the only trials Avey's journey requires. Having decided to abandon the tourist cruise, Avey is put ashore on Grenada, where, surrounded by her six cumbersome pieces of luggage, she begins to feel very much alone and afraid. Terrified by the unfamiliarity of her surroundings and by the fact that for some reason the people aren't even speaking English, but patois, Avey desperately wants to get on the first plane bound for New York. It is then out of great courage and in response to a very deep and urgent need that Avey decides to postpone her flight to security and undertakes another, more arduous journey that takes her deep into herself and her cultural past. Her guide through time is Lebert Joseph, who "saw how far she had come since leaving the ship and the distance she had yet to go" (*PSW*, 172) in her quest to redefine herself in race and culture. Together, they join the yearly migration of out-islanders from Grenada back to their small island home, Carriacou, where each will reunite with family members, pay homage to ancestors, and participate in the dances commemorating their African roots. The distance Avey has yet to go—the passage from Grenada to Carriacou—may be small in geographical terms, but it is vast when measured in personal suffering and psychic transformation.

During the course of her journey from cruise ship to Grenada to Carriacou, Avey is stripped of all the possessions that previously defined her middle-class life and values—the clothes, the coiffure, and finally the food. Overcome by seasickness, Avey undergoes a purge, first through a violent attack of vomiting, and then, an equally violent bout of diarrhea. The purge represents a symbolic break from bourgeois consumption and the transition to a very different relationship to food, defined not as a personal indulgence but as an object that articulates communal social relationships. On board the cruise ship, food, all of it heavy and rich, represented decadence, overabundance, and the impossibility of ever attaining individual satisfaction. In contrast, food on Carriacou represents a simple and wholesome repast for the living members of the community and a symbolic offering to its ancestors.

Avey's bout of sickness is finally more than a purge, for with the episodes of vomiting and diarrhea she is made to return to a particular childhood moment when she had also been sick and made a mess. The return to childhood is crucial to Avey's understanding of her present situation, because it forces her to reexamine the course of her life through the eyes of a child whose consciousness includes adult experience. The overlapping of child and adult is extremely important in Marshall's writing. We might take a line from *Brown Girl, Brownstones* as epigrammatic of the particular mode of consciousness Marshall brings to bear on her narrative. I refer to the moment when Suggie admonishes Selina for "spending [her] old days first" (*BGB*, 207). Selina's unique perspective on her household, which makes her wise beyond her years, is produced by Marshall's novelistic return to her own childhood, which gives her fiction the freshness of a child's vision and the depth of an adult's understanding. Avey Johnson's return to childhood represents, then, something of the same process the author undergoes in writing her fiction.

The Avey Johnson who emerges from the humiliating, body-weakening experience of seasickness awakens with fresh critical insight on her life. She comes to realize that the path from Halsey Street poverty to North White Plains respectability has not been a "natural" development, nor does it represent a desirable change. She comes to see, finally, that there is absolutely nothing "normal" about becoming bourgeois. This perspective on her life describes another important aspect of Marshall's writing: the inexorable scrutiny of those crucial moments in people's lives that finally define their development. In *Brown Girl, Brownstones*, Silla asks her daughter the critical question that Marshall will continue to demand of all her characters: "But who put you so?" (*BGB*, 192). As Selina discovers, and Avey Johnson, too, the answer to this question cannot be obtained by a simple review of personal history, because the personal is inextricably inscribed within the history of black people in this country. Going back to the formative, sometimes traumatic, moments of childhood sets the individual on the path of recovery in which the lessons gained by access to hindsight recast the child's experience in relation to the larger context of the history of the race.

When Avey Johnson is catapulted by vomiting and diarrhea into her childhood, she glimpses a vision, far more universal in its historical content and emblematic of the childhood of her race in the New World:

> It was nearing dusk and the *Emanuel C* was almost to port when the pall over Avey Johnson's mind lifted momentarily and she became dimly conscious. She was alone in the deckhouse. That much she was certain of. Yet she had the impression as her mind flickered on briefly of other bodies lying crowded in with her in the hot, airless dark. A multitude it felt like lay packed around her in the filth and stench of themselves, just as she was. Their moans, rising and falling with each rise and plunge of the schooner, enlarged upon the one filling her own head. Their suffering— the depth of it, the weight of it, in the cramped space— made hers of no consequence. (*PSW*, 209)

What is this dark, airless pit, packed with the moans and suffering of so many, but the hold of a slave ship? Avey, thrust upon the arc of recovery, has joined her people in the agony of the Middle Passage. Avey's return to the past (be it her childhood or that of her race) is no mere psychic journey, but one graphically etched on the physical senses, fusing her body and experience with that of the racial community. Throughout the novel, the history of slavery is recorded as a physical memory, something that can never be abstracted and therefore forgotten. When her great-aunt Cuney or Lebert Joseph take Avey by the wrist, she feels their hands as if they were "manacles," forcibly pulling her back into history, out of complacency and comfort, and thrusting her headlong into the awful brutality of her people's history. But for Avey, the manacles are the means for her salvation as is the Jack Iron rum Lebert uses to revive her after an overdose of tropic heat and sun. The book plays on the word "iron," using it as a grim reminder of slavery, which must be confronted and retrieved, and also the means for the individual's affirmation of self. The means for enslaving the black race becomes by reversal a metaphor articulating the individual's access to racial consciousness and liberation.

The strength of Marshall's images reside—as here—in their ability to evoke real bodily suffering. The individual's coming to consciousness coincides with deep physical involvement and only secondarily emerges with abstract thought and reflection. Marshall demonstrates that the translation back to the past need not be the subject of a sustained, chapter-length metaphor as it is in Octavia Butler's science-fiction novel, Kindred, [2] whose black protagonist is periodically projected out of her Los Angeles apartment and thrust into a pre–Civil War plantation where she experiences firsthand the realities of slavery. Rather, Marshall's paragraph-length transitions to the past produce singular, bold epiphanies, whose result is the discovery of the self—as black.

All of Marshall's novels pose the problem of how to narrate. Tracing the arc of recovery is for the author an interrogation into what constitutes the narrative. Avey's dream journey back to Tatem Island and her later passage to Carriacou bring to light many of the same issues related to the narrative and its community that Walter Benjamin discussed in his essay on storytelling.[3] Reacting against the fragmentation produced under modern capitalist society and responding to a nostalgia for older, traditional communities, Benjamin maintained that the possibility of having a story to tell in the first place is linked to the existence of an organic community and the individual's recognition of his or her place in the larger group. The story enacts experience and real experience can only be seen as such in a world not yet trivialized by all the forces associated with advanced capitalist society. Aunt Cuney's story of the slave ship that came one day to Tatem Island translates Benjamin's ideas into narrative. As she tells it, and as Avey later dreams it, the Africans took one look at the island and its plantation system and abruptly set off, chains and all, walking on the sea, back to Africa. The tale partakes of a narrative closure as spherical and complete as Tatem Island itself—not because it has a beginning, middle, and end—but because it articulates an event, which, for the people of Tatem Island, marked their identity. Cuney's grandmother, who as a young child witnessed the event, was in her lifetime the bearer of the tale. As Cuney remarks about her grandmother, "she just picked herself up and took off after 'em. In her mind. Her body she always usta say might be in Tatem but her mind, her mind was long gone with the Ibos . . . " (PSW, 39). If Cuney's grandmother is subsequently thought to be a little crazy by the rest of the community, it is their way of recognizing her lifelong relationship to the tale.

Similarly, Lebert Joseph, the community of Carriacou, and the dances commemorating the African nations represent a world still defined by storytelling. Here, narrative is enacted as ritual and dance; and the discourse is as tightly drawn as the fence line surrounding Lebert's yard, which contains the dancers. By comparison, Avey's North White Plains suburban life is defined by the absence of closure. Here, there is no community, no social whole whose individuals might be the bearers of a story. Rather than the singular events whose narration will forever constitute the individual's identity within the group, Avey's life has been the site of occasional memorable moments which, while they have defined her couple relationship, have not situated her in relation to a larger community. One of these is the moment she confronted her husband, Jay, for his acts of infidelity. This is the night it seemed Jay might leave for good, but chose instead to devote himself wholeheartedly to his wife, family, and job. No matter how important moments like these are in the life of an individual, they do not constitute the great narrative events as defined by Benjamin. Rather, like isolated moments in the amorphous flux of modern life, they explain an individual's relationship to a significant other, but they do not anchor either the individual or the couple in the larger organic identity of a group. For Avey, now a widow, her children grown, herself mired in the stifling security of her North White Plains home, the memories of married life and those drawn from the world of work cannot furnish meaningful stories. This is why the dream of her great-aunt Cuney has such a strong attraction and why the voyage to Carriacou cannot be denied.

What Lebert Joseph has, and Avey wishes she, too, might possess (although she knows she will never have it simply because her world has forgotten its cultural past), is "Li gain connaissance" (*PSW,* 218) This is Lebert's way of explaining his "special powers of seeing and knowing," which is analogous to the insight ascribed to Cuney's mythic Ibos, who, on arrival, were able to see all of slavery, the Civil War, "mancipation," and everything after that right on up to the hard times today (*PSW,* 38). At the heart of this worldview is the power to totalize experience. When Lebert Joseph asks Avey to name her "nation," he is asking her to define herself within a totality—something that Avey cannot do. Rather than totality, her life is composed of boring continuity: the kids at school, the ride downtown, the work in the office. In contrast, when Lebert Joseph closes down his rum shop to join the migration to Carriacou where he will dance his nation, he defines himself in relation to a cultural whole that makes a mockery of Avey's yearly migration on board the cruise ship. In dancing his nation, Lebert constitutes himself as the midpoint on an arc that reaches deep into the history of Africa and spans the New World and the new generations of black people who have immigrated to Canada and the States. In contrast, Avey's connections are partial, embracing no more than family members, and, like the telephone calls that link them, defined by an advanced technological society that abstracts and fragments human relationships.

Clearly, the desire for totality and the urgent need to invent a narrative capable of producing closure exist only for people who realize they no longer have totality in their lives but remember that such a state once existed. I think this summarizes Paule Marshall's position both as a writer and as an immigrant. Her writing is deeply haunted by the notion that there once existed a whole—the traditional Caribbean black community—but immigration and the pressures of life under commodity capitalism have sundered the whole. Her project as a writer is, then, to re-create the whole. Because Marshall views her own generation with despair for the plight of black people in the cities and disenchantment for the lives of blacks in the suburbs, recreating the whole means getting in touch with her mother's generation.

Marshall's novels enact the coming into being of social totality. This occurs in *Praisesong*, when, at the novel's conclusion, Avey joins her nation's dance, and in so doing, fuses her particular experience with the history of her race, her individual body with the community of dancers, all moving as one. Then, in *The Chosen Place, The Timeless People*, totality is recreated when the people of Bournehills stage their version of "Cuffee Ned's Revolt." This, their yearly offering to the island's carnival, is the only dramatization of an explicitly historical nature. As such, it is perceived as a contestatory statement by the island's more privileged classes. The masque recreates in history what Lebert Joseph's dance of the nation accomplishes in culture; that is, the redefinition of scattered, daily experience in terms of a totality. The enactment of Cuffee Ned's attack on the plantation owner and the months he spent as an outlaw speak to the present history of the people of Bournehills, who continue to live under a modified plantation system, but whose open defiance manifests the spirit of maroonage.[4] When the Cuffee Ned float joins the carnival parade, it brings with it a host of chanting Bournehills people, all singing, all dancing as one. Their communal zeal infests the crowd of spectators and produces, in very energetic terms, the deep and binding sense of community that Marshall so often strives to convey.

The effort to totalize is all the more striking since the collective memory, as Marshall records it, involves a multiplicity of historical views. In fact, the people of Bournehills have been known to come to blows over questions of history: did Cuffee Ned hold out for three months, six months, or was it nine months before he was finally captured and hung? The problem Marshall is grappling with is not which version is finally correct, but how to portray a community as both multidimensional (possessed of many experiences and many meanings) and at the same time allow this community to be seen as the coherent center and source for black self-definition. On the one hand is the reality that communities in the modern Third World are not conveniently homogenized social units as they are often imaged to be from the First World point of view. And on the other hand is the strong desire on the part of an immigrant artist and intellectual living in the First World to somehow give meaning to her life and work (as well as that of all Afro-Americans) in relation to an ancestral home and culture. In *The Chosen Place, The Timeless People*, Marshall avoids the temptation to evoke a false sense of daily unity among the people of Bournehills, but demonstrates how the multiplicity of their points of view is, then, drawn up during the carnival to produce a single, communal version of history. Performance totalizes the multiplicity, and so too does Marshall's narrative.

It is important to bear in mind that the function of the narrative runs counter to the oral tradition that Marshall's novels want to preserve and at the same time draw on as the source of their meaning. When Benjamin says that traditional societies are defined by storytelling, he does not imply that villages must agree on specific story versions. Furthermore, his notion of closure does not assume that every story must have a beginning, middle, and end. Rather, village storytellers are often interrupted, their tales intersected by diverse experiential bits. What the novel does is to integrate these bits into a narrative whole, situating them according to the demands of causality and temporality. Marshall, in seeking out the source of her cultural identity, confronts a multiplicity that the novel (particularly her more realist version of the novel) cannot reproduce. The process of writing a novel may well represent the application of a system of meaning and telling originating in dominant culture to a body of narrative raw material Marshall hopes will yield an alternative perspective on the culture of domination. This makes Marshall's writing an enterprise fraught with contradiction. It may well be that neither Tatem Island, nor Bournehills, nor Carriacou are actually the sites out of which meaning emanates, but they are defined as such by the novelistic form and by the author's ardent desire to render culture whole.

By comparison, *Brown Girl, Brownstones* lacks the notion of totality. Rather than a Tatem Island or a Bournehills community, it offers the sadly dystopian image of the Barbadian Association, whose stuffy meetings and bourgeois values make this the antithesis of the vital Third World community portrayed in Marshall's other novels. But the lack of a totalizing culture source does not make *Brown Girl, Brownstones* a lesser novel. In fact, I'd say it is a far more interesting book precisely because it articulates the formal characteristics of modernism (see chapter 1) and does not seek out historically and culturally distant islands of totalizing experience. Rather than attempting narrative closure, this is a novel composed of anecdotes. There is no one single event whose telling can then constitute either Selina's identity or that of her neighbors. Instead, there are many separate but related stories whose telling defines a family, a household, a neighborhood. Miss Thompson, whose life-sore testifies to her narrow escape from rape, represents one story; Suggie, indolent and sensual, is another; and Miss Mary, her mind a reservoir of old tales and telling, represents yet another story. Selina's life is a process of bringing together all these storytellers— visiting them, listening to them, and stringing together their separate experiences in the fabric of her growing up. But this does not produce narrative closure simply because no one story—nor all the stories taken together—can be totalizing in Selina's world where immigration and industrialization have created a fragmented social composite rather than an organic whole. The brilliance of this novel is its recognition that all of the separate stories did at one time and in their specific historical contexts function as totalizing narratives: Miss Thompson's tale for the rural South, Suggie's for Barbadian peasant society, and Miss Mary's for the bygone era of the nineteenth-century white bourgeoisie. But severed from their historical moments and social contexts, these tales—like the immigrants who tell them—no longer have the power to totalize. The great adventure recorded in *Brown Girl, Brownstones* and the reason for its sensitive treatment of Selina's personal anguish, is rooted in the understanding that totalizing is no longer possible. Selina is a brave and interesting character precisely because she cannot undertake a quest to uproot some bygone era (as Avey does), but must, instead, wrest a sense of personal integrity and mission from among the shattered bits of her experience and the social rubble that surrounds her.

In Selina's growing up there is a single voice whose function is not to tell anecdotes—but to admonish, threaten, taunt, and cajole. This is the voice of her mother, which fills up and takes possession of domestic space in such a way that both Selina and her father often have to retreat to some isolated corner—usually the sun porch—there to dream of the past and ponder improbable futures. The mother's voice, given in fragmented bits, smacks of persistent care, continuity in the face of great change, an enduring presence whose strength is felt even when she is out of the house at work:

> But look at he. Tha's one man don know his own mind. He's always looking for something big and praying hard not to find it. (*BGB*, 21)

> But look at she! She's nothing but a living dead. She been down here since they said "Come let us make woman." She might pass on and pass away and make room in the world for somebody else. (*BGB*, 19)

> That concubine don know shame. Here it tis she just come to this man country and every time you look she got a different man ringing down the bell... (*BGB*, 17)

> Poor Thompson. Somebody mussa put she so that she does break down work to support somebody else's wild-dog puppies, instead of taking care of the life-sore 'pon she foot. (*BGB*, 27)

These are Silla's pronouncements on her husband, Miss Mary, Suggie, and Miss Thompson. They capture the rhythm of the black household and the voice of maternal wisdom. These are the sort of refrains that Marshall herself heard as a child, in her mother's kitchen when friends and neighbors gathered to comment on the life and morality of the neighborhood. Steeped in folk wisdom, these refrains are Selina's bridge to a sense of a past Barbadian culture, which will never be totally hers, and a present community of sharing among women, which can be hers as she grows to adulthood.

One of the major problems facing black writers today is how to preserve the black cultural heritage in the face of the homogenizing function of bourgeois society. This is a problem particularly relevant to black women writers, who, as mothers, are more apt to see the loss of a sense of black history and culture in their children. For today's black women writers, the project of reclaiming history, although it may have its culmination in African culture, is more precisely aimed at a retrieval of the twenties, thirties, and early forties. This is the era of jazz, blues, and the poetry of Langston Hughes. But how to retrieve the past without making its artifacts the museum pieces of the eighties? Marshall attempts to solve the problem by evoking a family context—the image of Jay and Avey tripping the light fantastic in their tenement living room, to the recorded music of "Take the A-Train" or "Stompin' at the Savoy," or Jay reciting "Little brown baby wif spa'klin / eyes" to his own little brown babies. But because these are by now recognized culture pieces and because no author—no matter how imbued in the culture of the past—can really bring the whole context of the past into the present, these references are infused with a sort of dead cultural weight, which the voice of Selina's mother escapes. Charged with vitality and the timelessness of domestic travail, it summons up a past in its atonal Barbadian accent and puts the reader in touch with the 1940s New York black neighborhood.

More than the general influence of commodity culture on the urban black family, Marshall's focus is acutely aimed at the transition of the American black population from a lumpen and working-class background to professional and middle-class standing. Both Toni Morrison in *Song of Solomon* and Paule Marshall in *Brown Girl, Brownstones* show that the process of integration into the bourgeoisie is intimately bound up with land ownership. The driving force that transforms Milkman's father from a homeless refugee from the countryside to a Detroit city slumlord is the same driving force that captures Marshall's Bajan community, instilling each of its members with the relentless desire to "buy house." In *Brown Girl, Brownstones*, the pursuit of private property becomes an overwhelming desire, supplanting all other passions including the sexual. Why this is so has a lot to do with the way the immigrant Barbadian population confronted and dealt with the systems of race and class they found in this country. On their arrival, the Barbadians ran head-on into a system of professional segregation that meant service-sector employment for black men and women. Education and access to the professions merely created parallel employment and institutions for blacks. This is the hard lesson Selina's father learns, when, having completed his studies in accounting, he is denied employment in white firms by reason of race. Only those black professionals who established "separate but equal" enterprises in the black neighborhood would be allowed to succeed. The Barbadians' struggle to become property owners represents a mode of self-affirmation precisely as it is articulated in a society that prevents integration in the workplace. The advent of the Second World War greatly changed the social position of many urban blacks. As Marshall documents it, the war opened the factories to black women, lifting them out of domestic daywork, giving them a salary and making them a part of the proletariat. However, elevation to factory work came at a time when the immigrant Barbadian population was already hell-bent on acquiring property. Thus, rather than radicalizing them, it more securely bound the Barbadians to bourgeois class aspirations based on property ownership.

Marshall demonstrates deep political understanding in *Brown Girl, Brownstones* by showing that the desire to own property may well have represented an initial contestation of bourgeois white domination, but because property ownership is implicit in capitalist society, the moment of opposition was immediately absorbed and integrated into the context of American capitalism. As long as white property owners could move out to the suburbs, it mattered little—nor did it represent a transformation of the system—that black people might be establishing parallel property systems in the cities. Marshall shows great sensitivity in demonstrating how the desire for property is lived as a passion, whose result is the repression of sexuality and the transformation of a loving, supportive couple relationship into one defined by deceit and treachery. Marshall's great talent as a writer is to show how broad historical developments are lived by families—and particularly by women in their roles as daughters and mothers. When we read *Brown Girl, Brownstones*, we cannot help but be amazed at the power of Silla's desire to "buy house," to be a full citizen like her neighbors, who, on their way up and out of poverty, ape middle-class modes of behavior. We cannot help but be struck by the horrible dissension the mother's project unleashes, which has its culmination in Silla's betrayal of her husband and Selina's denunciation of her mother as a "Hitler." And finally, we cannot help but be dumbfounded at Silla's brutal denial of self—her self-sacrifice, never allowing herself a moment's frivolity; her toil, taking on long hours and difficult jobs; and finally her repression of sexuality. Her refusal to have sex with her husband seems all the more self-negating when we see Silla, as Marshall portrays her during a wedding reception, dancing with delightful abandon and deep sensuality. Caught up in the all-consuming obsession to save every nickel and dime and to convert her husband's piece of land in Barbados into a down payment on a New York brownstone, Silla becomes a living embodiment of compulsive desires, some of which (like her frugality and possessiveness) she probably inherited with her peasant origins, but all of which dovetail with the demands of capitalism. The beauty of Marshall's portrayal is to make us ever aware of Silla's deeply human passions, which have been repressed or distorted in her relentless drive to ascend to the middle class.

By comparison to Silla, both Deighton, her husband, and Suggie, her lodger, represent alternative social modes whose oppositionality to bourgeois society must, by the very nature of capitalism, be shown to be counterproductive and therefore improper. Thus Suggie, who uses sex to negate her loneliness and the despair of domestic work, is defined by Silla as a "concubine," a ne'er-do-well, and finally, an expendable being. Similarly, Deighton, whose entire life articulates strategies of "how-not-to-succeed-in-business-while-really-trying," is, by Silla's reprimands labeled frivolous, irresponsible, and also expendable. Silla's unrelenting cruelty in evicting Suggie and causing her husband's deportation and eventual death, ought not be seen as personal vendettas. Rather, both articulate the power and fundamental nature of capitalism as it takes possession of people's lives. From this point of view, Silla's actions represent rational solutions to counterproductive forces. Again, the power of Marshall's writing lies in her ability to define, on the one hand, the political motivations behind Silla's acts of cruelty, while at the same time showing that Silla really is not a monster, but a highly conflicted individual whose passions and desires have all been distorted by her integration into white bourgeois capitalism.

In *Brown Girl, Brownstones* and *The Chosen Place, The Timeless People* there is a strange and striking similarity between two characters who by reason of their race and class ought to have nothing in common—namely, Silla, the Barbadian immigrant, and Harriet, the blue-blooded Yankee, both of whom fabricate elaborate strategies of deceit involving behind-the-scenes letter writing in order to achieve a goal that is both personal and material. There is no way to explain their actions or the similarity between Silla and Harriet except by reference to the influence of capitalism on couple relationships—and particularly on women's psychology. Silla writes fraudulent letters to her sister-in-law over a period of many months and eventually achieves the sale of her husband's land. Harriet's letters go to her rich uncle who controls her husband's development project. Her goal is to have her husband replaced as head of the fieldwork so that the two of them can return to a comfortable bourgeois life in the States. Both women enact strategies of chicanery typically ascribed to women, whose positions of inferiority in relation to male-dominated institutions tend to transcend race and class distinctions.

But Marshall's sense of the situation goes deeper, to probe beyond motivations anchored in sexism. As she portrays them, both women act out of a deeply tormented and highly possessive love for their husbands. Both feel they might be losing their husbands—Deighton drifting off into frivolity and indolence, and Saul absorbed more and more by his work and his growing concern for the people of Bournehills. Both women act to contain, to domesticate, if you will, male energy, which, as Marshall portrays it, tends to diverge from the women's expectations. Both women represent a conservative force, and in the context of this portrayal of women, Selina emerges as an extremely interesting character whose growing up is made all the more difficult by the fact that she seeks to break out of the domestic, property-oriented role traditionally ascribed to women. As the book depicts them, the male figures, Clive, the Bohemian, and Deighton, the spendthrift, are the radical figures, whereas the women, Silla and her neighbors, represent morality and progress. By comparison, Selina represents the emergence of a new and critical perspective on adult society. Neither a social misfit like her father nor a social bastion like her mother, Selina accepts the difficult position of being ever questioning of herself and others and at the same time acts out of responsibility to self and others.

The similarity between Harriet and Silla ends abruptly on the point of Harriet's racism. Whereas Silla's deceit is in some way motivated by the desire to overcome racist society, Harriet's actions are largely motivated by her hatred and fear of black people. Swept away with the carnival merrymakers, Harriet comes face-to-face with her racist sentiments. Actually, her fear and loathing for black people had always lurked below the surface of her condescension and philanthropy. Her desire to wrest her husband away from Bournehills is finally motivated by the disgust she feels on discovering that Saul has had an affair with Merle, a black woman. Harriet, as the symbolic embodiment of old-style Yankee capitalism, demonstrates that deceit is a tool for maintaining class power. And as a class, the bourgeoisie is quite capable of betraying loved ones, particularly when their activities run counter to the demands of domination. Saul's lack of racist sentiments and his ability to organize the people of Bournehills into self-determining production units make him an enemy of capitalism. Moreover, as a class, the bourgeoisie is quite capable of committing crimes against an entire community. This is the symbolic thrust of Harriet's desire to withdraw the funding and the field chief from the Bournehills project.

These, then, are modes of behavior evolved with white domination and bourgeois class authority. In her headlong drive to acquire property, Silla not only buys into the bourgeoisie, but into its modes of behavior as well. This is not to suggest that black peasant women are incapable of manipulative behavior or that they learn how to betray loved ones only by contagion with the white world. On the contrary, as Marshall shows, the practice of Obeah has traditionally been the black woman's means of manipulating power. The difference between sorcery and bourgeois deceit is the high degree of abstraction that informs the latter. The calculated brand of betrayal practiced by Silla and Harriet speaks for a transformation in human relationships that occurs under capitalism and transforms human beings into objects capable of being perceived as obstructions to progress.

The influence of capitalism as a lived experience, particularly as it shapes the middle class, is most evident in Marshall's descriptions of domestic space and—not surprisingly—women's bodies. Both are, in fact, depicted as constructs, wherein the shell of the body, like the shell of the home, is shown to be the container of all the tensions and cares produced in daily life. In *Praisesong*, Avey's traveling companion, Clarice, whose weight has increased with each familial crisis, "the fat metastasizing with each new sorrow" (*PSW*, 24) epitomizes the self-condemning body of guilt. In capitalist society, the use of food as a compensatory satisfaction cuts across class lines and includes many disparate groups including middle-class teenage girls and white working-class middle-age women. Clarice, who by reason of race ought not be susceptible to the pathologies that haunt the white world, has nevertheless been assimilated to white society by reason of her aspirations for social advancement. Her greatest blow and the deepest cause of her social sorrow was her son's decision to drop out of a predominantly white college where he had been a straight A student. The root of Clarice's dissatisfaction, which impels her to seek gratification in sweets and compulsive eating, is analogous to the driving force behind Silla's obsessive desire to "buy house." Both women desire upward social mobility, with the white bourgeois life-style their model of social perfection. When Clarice's son thwarts his mother's social aspirations, her desire is not dispelled, but finding no alternative outlet in capitalist society, she has nowhere to turn but into hollow consumption. This is how capitalist society works to deflect the energies and passions of people who would otherwise pose a potential threat. Clarice, her shoulders sloping, her body bloated, her spirit cowed, is the grotesque embodiment of capitalism's strategy for perpetuating a society defined by the barriers of class and race. As long as there are false gratifications—and the glut of consumer society shows no sign of diminishing—the Clarices of this world will always be appeased, their bodies the sign of their appeasement.

For Silla, in *Brown Girl, Brownstones*, the desire for upward social mobility is thwarted by her husband. Finding no alternative channel in bourgeois society, her passion spirals inward, generating deep hatred aimed not at a dominant society but at her own husband. When Silla finally does acquire a brownstone, sacrificing her spirit and her sensuality for a mortgage, the house, like Clarice's body, becomes her prison. Caught up in the need for ever more income (her desire for accumulation equal to Clarice's need to consume), Silla becomes a landlady, beseiged by a host of poverty-stricken tenants, her own imprisoning fat cells. Similarly, Avey Johnson's home in *Praisesong* is the sign of her appeasement. Although her middle-class standing precludes Avey's ever having to be a landlady, she is, nevertheless, just as imprisoned by her home as Silla. Held captive by the dark and heavy security of the house, longing for her china and silver, Avey is entombed in a bourgeois stability whose hallmark is property ownership. Her spirit—and with it the quest for an alternative mode of living—has been negated, transformed into a museum piece like all the objects housed in her North White Plains home.

The great liberating power of Avey's trip to Carriacou derives from its ability to reveal the deadening oppression of bourgeois security. Only by passing through the mind-quickening experience of retrieving African culture can Avey come to see how empty and limiting life in the suburbs had been. Avey's subsequent vision of an alternative future, which involves rebuilding her great-aunt's house and making it into a summer home for wayward city kids and her own grandchildren, suggests a liberal, reformist notion of how to bring about social change. Although it might have been more interesting had Avey emerged from her Carriacou experience with a more revolutionary notion of a future society, Marshall's lack of a radical political vision is less important than her implicit understanding that bourgeois society as it has been defined by white domination must be broken with and eliminated. This is not the case for those elements from Avey's past that define her black cultural heritage even though these have evolved in the context of white domination. Her husband's music and her great-aunt's stories constitute the lines of continuity with the past and are themselves remembered and reborn as Avey begins to put aside her middle-class concerns and objects.

In all of Marshall's novels, the transformation out of bourgeois encumbrances and values is enacted physically on the bodies of her female characters. The body provides a medium for metaphors of history, making these metaphors experientially concrete. This is another reason why we as readers tend to experience Marshall's characters as deeply human, capable of generating approximations to our own physically encoded feelings and experiences. When, after her bout of seasickness, Avey finally sheds her long-line girdle and yields her rippled and complacently fat thighs to Lebert's daughter who massages and bathes her, we, too, experience the initial inhibitions of her flesh. We understand how years of middle-class comfort laid down the fat cells and how the particular inactivity associated with commuting and secretarial work kept the fat there. And we realize, along with Avey, how her husband's gradual inattention, concerned more with his work than with simple sensual pleasures, conditioned Avey to become unaware of her own body. Feeling the masseuse's penetrating fingertips, Avey recognizes her body's long and numbing entombment; and with her mind's eye, she comes to see how dark and imprisoning her house has been.

Traversing the arc of recovery involves, then, bursting through the constraints associated with bourgeois complacency. This is why dance is fundamentally important in Marshall's writing. The brief moment when Silla dances at Gatha Steed's wedding party, she uses her body to explode all her self-imposed restraints. Dancing, Silla reveals her vibrant sensuality and sparklingly happy nature, which have been repressed in her body-numbing and soul-stifling drive to buy a house. Similarly,

Selina uses modern dance to get at the place where her soul resides. Dance, whether it be the timeless dance of the nations or
the free-form patterns of modern dance, has the power to lift the
individual out of socially encoded formulas, substituting its abstract form for the ensnaring patterns of daily life. Dance is also
the means for Avey's liberation. Once having mastered the precise rhythm and movement of the Carriacou shuffle, she understands that her body is no longer the container of her personal
desires and wants, but the articulation of her people's collective
history.

Merle, from *The Chosen Place, The Timeless People*, is Marshall's atypical character, for whom dance is not a means for either the liberation of the self or the discovery of the community.
Her every movement a staccato action, her talk incessant, her
body hectic, Merle is the embodiment of deep frustration.
Rather than complacently accepting the guilt born of social contradiction as Clarice has done, Merle has experimented with radical politics and choses to confront the landowners of the world.
Although middle-aged, her breasts beginning to droop, her upper
arms to shudder, and her face to slacken, Merle, as Marshall portrays her, is neither entombed by her body nor by her age. What
ensnares Merle is something much larger than the middle-class
life-style that stifles so many of Marshall's characters. What
Merle is up against is the entire history of colonialism that defined black people as plantation slaves and made Merle a
twentieth-century bastard, the daughter of a white landowner.
The colonial system continues to shape not only the economy
and daily life of all of Bournehills, but also Merle's attempts to
transform her life whether in London or at home. Merle's every
moment is, thus, the articulation of the frenzied desire for real
confrontation, held always in check because in neo-imperialist
relationships, real authority resides outside of the colony and
very often presents only the diffuse facade of the multinational.
Merle's attempt to square off with the owner of the sugar mill
leads to her deeper frustration, since it is clear that the pompous

old man who owns the mill represents authority only in the colony. He, like the white journalist and black lawyer, are stand-ins for the invisible centers of power that Merle will never be able to confront. In the context of the failure to produce confrontation and resolution, Merle is unable to enact her self-recovery through dance or other forms of cultural practice. Rather, catatonia is her mode of self-retrieval. In this, she is very like Walker's Meridian, the Civil Rights activist, who, after each confrontation with white authority, also collapses into deep spells of catatonia. Rather than a mode of retreat, catatonia is for these characters a zone for the restoration of self, a separate plateau from which the body and spirit emerge to once again take up the fight.

Tracing the arc of recovery becomes, then, a project for reclaiming the individual, and thereby affirming the continuity of Afro-Americans as a whole. It may be that all three of Marshall's soul-searching women characters—Selina, Merle, and Avey—have their inception in Marshall's reaction against an epithet she undoubtedly encountered in Jean Toomer's *Cane*. For here, in this brilliant and soul-searchingly tormented novel, is another Avey, one described as an "orphan Woman."[5] Toomer portrays his Avey as wantonly indolent—forever drifting, unaware of her past, and never questioning her future. She is the embodiment of her creator's own conflicted relationship to race, which caused Toomer in the early part of his life to define himself as black and later, after the publication of *Cane*, to pass for white. Marshall's Avey (and her Selina and Merle as well) are written against the forces in this society that attempt to eliminate the black cultural identity, and, finally, black people. In reclaiming her women characters as selves, she constitutes them—no longer as individuals—but as figures for the continuation of community.

4. Eruptions of Funk

Historicizing Toni Morrison

"I begin to feel those little bits of color floating up into me—deep in me. That streak of green from the june-bug light, the purple from the berries trickling along my thighs. Mama's lemonade yellow runs sweet in me. Then I feel like I'm laughing between my legs, and the laughing gets all mixed up with the colors, and I'm afraid I'll come, and afraid I won't. But I know I will. And I do. And it be rainbow all inside." (*TBE*, 103–4)

This is the way Polly Breedlove in *The Bluest Eye* remembers the experience of orgasm—*remembers* it, because in the grim and shabby reality of her present, orgasm (which we might take as a metaphor for any deeply pleasurable experience) is no longer possible.[1] Living in a storefront, her husband fluctuating between brutality and apathy, her son estranged, her daughter just plain scared, Polly has no language to describe the memory of a past pleasure, except one drawn from her distant childhood.

The power of this passage is not just related to the fact that it evokes the most intense female experience possible. Much of the impact is produced by the way it describes. Morrison defamiliarizes the portrayal of sensual experience. Adjectives become substantives, giving taste to color and making it possible for colors to trickle and flow and, finally, to be internalized like the semen of an orgasmic epiphany.

As often happens in Morrison's writing, sexuality converges

with history and functions as a register for the experience of change, i.e., historical transition. Polly's remembrance of childhood sensuality coincides with her girlhood in the rural South. Both are metaphorically condensed and juxtaposed with the alienation she experiences as a black emigrant and social lumpen in a Northern industrial city. The author's metaphoric language produces an estrangement of alienation. Although her metaphors are less bold in their form and content, they still achieve an effect very similar to that of the negritude poets. Indeed, the image of an internal rainbow evokes the poetics of surrealism, but in a language less disjunctive because prose reveals the historical and artistic process through which the image is produced.[2]

When Polly Breedlove reminisces, her present collides with her past and spans her family's migration from the hills of Alabama to a small Kentucky town and her own subsequent journey as the wife of one of the many black men who, in the late thirties and early forties, sought factory jobs in the industrial North. The rural homeland is the source of the raw material of experience and praxis, which in the border-state small town is abstracted to colors, tastes, and tactile sensations. Ohio is, then, the site where images are produced out of the discontinuity between past and present.

Neither Morrison's use of metaphor, nor her general drive to return to origins is rooted in a nostalgia for the past. Rather, the metaphoric rendition of past experience represents a process for coming to grips with historical transition. Migration to the North signifies more than a confrontation with (and contamination by) the white world. It implies a transition in social class. Throughout Morrison's writing, the white world is equated with the bourgeois class—its ideology and life-style. This is true of *Song of Solomon* in which Macon Dead's attitudes toward rents and property make him more "white" than "black." This is true of *Tar Baby* in which notions of bourgeois morality and attitudes concerning the proper education and role of women have created a contemporary "tar baby," a black woman in cultural limbo. And it is made dramatically clear in *The Bluest Eye*, whose epigrammatic introduction and subsequent chapter headings are drawn from a white, middle-class "Dick-and-Jane" reader. In giving voice to the experience of growing up black in a society dominated by white, middle-class ideology, Morrison is writing against the privatized world of suburban house and nuclear family, whose social and psychological fragmentation does not need her authorial intervention, but is aptly portrayed in the language of the reader: "Here is the family. Mother, Father, Dick, and Jane live in the green-and-white house. They are very happy" (*TBE*, 7).

The problem at the center of Morrison's writing is how to maintain an Afro-American cultural heritage once the relationship to the black rural South has been stretched thin over distance and generations. Although a number of black Americans will criticize her problematizing of Afro-American culture, seeing in it a symptom of Morrison's own relationship to white bourgeois society as a successful writer and editor, there are a number of social and historical factors that argue in support of her position. These include the dramatic social changes produced by recent wide-scale migration of industry to the South, which has transformed much of the rural population into wage laborers; the development, particularly in the Northern cities, of a black bourgeoisie; and the coming into being, under late capitalism, of a full-blown consumer society capable of homogenizing society by recouping cultural difference. The temporal focus of each of Morrison's novels pinpoints strategic moments in black American history during which social and cultural forms underwent disruption and transformation. Both *The Bluest Eye* and *Sula* focus on the forties, a period of heavy black migration to the cities, when, particularly in the Midwest, black "neighborhoods" came into being as annexes of towns that had never before had a sizable black population. *Sula* expands the period of the forties by looking back to the First World War, when blacks as a social group were first incorporated into a modern capitalist system as soldiers, and it looks ahead to the sixties, when cultural identity seems to flatten out, and, as Helene Sabat observes, all young people tend to look like the "Deweys," the book's nameless and indistinguishable orphans. *Song of Solomon* focuses on the sixties, when neighborhoods are perceived from the outside and called ghettos, a time of urban black political activism and general countercultural awareness. And *Tar Baby*, Morrison's most recent book, is best characterized as a novel of the eighties, in which the route back to cultural origins is very long and tenuous, making many individuals cultural exiles.

With this as an outline of modern black history in the United States, Morrison develops the social and psychological aspects that characterize the lived experience of historical transition. For the black emigrant to the North, the first of these is alienation. As Morrison defines it, alienation is not simply the result of an individual's separation from his or her cultural center, although this is a contributory factor that reinforces the alienation produced by the transition to wage labor. For the black man incorporated into the wartime labor pool (as for many white Appalachians),[3] selling one's labor for the creation of surplus value was only half of alienation, whose brutal second half was the grim reality of unemployment once war production was no longer necessary. The situation for the black woman was somewhat different. Usually employed as a maid and therefore only marginally incorporated as a wage laborer, her alienation was the result of striving to achieve the white bourgeois social model (in which she worked but did not live), which is itself produced by the system of wage labor under capitalism. As housemaid in a prosperous lakeshore home, Polly Breedlove lives a form of schizophrenia, in which her marginality is constantly confronted with a world of Hollywood movies, white sheets, and tender blond children. When at work or at the movies, she separates herself from her own kinky hair and decayed tooth. The tragedy of a woman's alienation is its effect on her role as mother. Her emotions split, Polly showers tenderness and love on her employer's child, and rains violence and disdain on her own.

Morrison's aim in writing is very often to disrupt alienation with what she calls eruptions of "funk" (*TBE*, 68). Dismayed by the tremendous influence of bourgeois society on young black women newly arrived from deep South cities like "Meridian, Mobile, Aiken and Baton Rouge," Morrison describes the women's loss of spontaneity and sensuality. They learn "how to behave. The careful development of thrift, patience, high morals, and good manners. In short, how to get rid of the funkiness. The dreadful funkiness of passion, the funkiness of nature, the funkiness of the wide range of human emotions" (*TBE*, 68).

For Polly Breedlove, alienation is the inability to experience pleasure ever again—orgasm or otherwise—whereas for the "sugar-brown Mobile girls" (*TBE*, 68), whose husbands are more successful and therefore better assimilated into bourgeois society, alienation is the purposeful denial of pleasure. Once again Morrison translates the loss of history and culture into sexual terms and demonstrates the connection between bourgeois society and repression:

> He must enter her surreptitiously, lifting the hem of her nightgown only to her navel. He must rest his weight on his elbows when they make love, ostensibly to avoid hurting her breasts but actually to keep her from having to touch or feel too much of him.
>
> While he moves inside her, she will wonder why they didn't put the necessary but private parts of the body in some more convenient place—like the armpit, for example, or the palm of the hand. Someplace one could get to easily, and quickly, without undressing. She stiffens when she feels one of her paper curlers coming undone from the activity of love; imprints in her mind which one it is that is coming loose so she can quickly secure it once he is

through. She hopes he will not sweat—the damp may get into her hair; and that she will remain dry between her legs—she hates the glucking sound they make when she is moist. When she senses some spasm about to grip him, she will make rapid movements with her hips, press her fingernails into his back, suck in her breath, and pretend she is having an orgasm. (*TBE*, 69)

At a sexual level, alienation is the denial of the body, produced when sensuality is redefined as indecent. Sounds and tactile sensations that might otherwise have precipitated or highlighted pleasure provoke annoyance or disdain. Repression manifests itself in the fastidious attention given to tomorrow's Caucasian-inspired coiffure and the decathexis of erogenous stimulation. Although repression inhibits sexual pleasure, it does not liberate a woman from sexuality. In faking an orgasm, the woman negates her pleasure for the sake of her husband's satisfaction, thus defining herself as a tool of his sexual gratification.

To break through repressed female sexuality, Morrison contrasts images of stifled womanhood with girlhood sensuality. In *The Bluest Eye*, the author's childhood alter ego, Claudia, is fascinated by all bodily functions and the physical residues of living in the world. She rebels at being washed, finding her scrubbed body obscene due to its "dreadful and humiliating absence of dirt" (*TBE*, 21). Even vomit is interesting for its color and consistency as it "swaddles down the pillow onto the sheet" (*TBE*, 13). In wondering how anything can be "so neat and nasty at the same time" (*TBE*, 13), Claudia shows a resistance toward the overdetermination of sensual experience, which, as Morrison sees it, is the first step toward repression. Openness to a full range of sensual experience may be equated with polymorphous sexuality, typified by the refusal of many young children to be thought of as either a boy or a girl. As my own four-year-old daughter sees it, "Little girls grow up to be big boys," and because there is no firm distinction between the sexes, her teddy bear is "both a boy and a girl." The refusal to categorize sensual experience—and likewise sex—captures the essence of unre-pressed childhood, which Morrison evokes as a mode of exist-ence prior to the individual's assimilation into bourgeois society.

The ultimate horror of bourgeois society against which Morri-son writes and the end result of both alienation and repression is reification.[4] None of Morrison's black characters actually ac-cedes to the upper reaches of bourgeois reification, but there are some who come close. They are saved only because they remain marginal to the bourgeois class and are imperfectly assimilated to bourgeois values. In *Song of Solomon*, Hagar offers a good ex-ample. Rejected by her lover, she falls into a state of near-catatonia, oblivious to all around her. However, chancing to look in a mirror, she is horrified by her appearance and marvels that anyone could love a woman with her looks. Thus roused from her withdrawal, Hagar embarks on a daylong shopping spree, driven by the desire to be the delightful image promised by her brand-name purchases:

> She bought a Playtex garter belt, I. Miller No Color hose, Fruit of the Loom panties, and two nylon slips—one white, one pink—one pair of Joyce Fancy Free and one of Con Brio ("Thank heaven for little Joyce heels"). . . .
> The cosmetics department enfolded her in perfume, and she read hungrily the labels and the promise. Myrurgia for primeval woman who creates for him a world of tender pri-vacy where the only occupant is you, mixed with Nina Ric-ci's L'Air du Temps. Yardley's Flair with Tuvaché's Nectaroma and D'Orsay's Intoxication. (*SOS*, 314–15)

Hagar's shopping spree culminates in a drenching downpour. Her shopping bags soaked, everything—her "Sunny Glow" and "fawn-trimmed-in-sea-foam shortie nightgown"—her wished-for identity and future—falls into the wet and muddy street. Re-turning home, Hagar collapses with fever and dies after days of delirium.

Hagar's hysteria and death mark the limits of her assimilation into bourgeois culture. Neither through withdrawal nor through commodity consumption can Hagar transform herself into an object. Her marginality, by reason of race and lumpen background, is the basis for her inalienable human dimension. As Morrison might have put it, she is simply too black, too passionate, too human ever to become reified.

Reification, although never attained by any of Morrison's characters—not even those drawn from the white world[5]—is, instead, embodied in a number of figural images from *The Bluest Eye.* These are the celluloid images of Shirley Temple or her "cu-ute" face on a blue-and-white china cup, and the candy-wrapper images of Mary Jane. Most of all, reification is evident in the plastic smile and moronic blue eyes of a white Christmas baby doll. When Claudia destroys these—dismembering the doll and poking its eyes out—her rebellion is not just aimed at the idea of beauty incarnated in a white model. She is also striking out against the horrifying dehumanization that acceptance of the model implies—both for the black who wears it as a mask and for the white who creates commodified images of the self.

For Morrison, everything is historical; even objects are embedded in history and are the bearers of the past. For those characters closest to the white bourgeois world, objects contain the residues of repressed and unrealized desires. For Ruth Foster in *Song of Solomon,* the daughter of the town's first black doctor and wife of the slumlord Macon Dead, a watermark on a table is the stubborn and ever-present reminder of her husband's remorseless rejection. The bowl of flowers around which their hatred crystallized is no longer present; only its sign remains, an opaque residue indelibly written into the table. If, for the bourgeois world, experience is capable of being abstracted to the level of sign, this is not the case for the world of the marginal characters. To cite another example from *Song of Solomon,* Pilate, Ruth Foster's sister-in-law and in every way her antithesis, enjoys a special relationship to all levels of natural experience—including a specific shade of blue sky. Now, color does not function as a sign in the way that the watermark on the table does. Although it bears a concrete relationship to a real object (the blue ribbons on Pilate's mother's hat), it is not an abstract relationship in the way that the watermark stands for the bowl of flowers. For Ruth Foster, the watermark is an "anchor" to the mental and sexual anguish imprisoned in the sign. In contrast, when Pilate points to a patch of sky and remarks that it is the same color as her mother's bonnet ribbons, she enables her nephew Milkman (Ruth Foster's overly sheltered son) to experience a unique moment of sensual perception. The experience is liberational because Pilate is not referring to a specific bonnet— or even to a specific mother; rather, the color blue triggers the whole range of emotions associated with maternal love, which Pilate offers to anyone who will share the experience of color with her.

In contrast to the liberational aspect of *Song of Solomon*, Morrison's most recent novel, *Tar Baby*, registers a deep sense of pessimism. Here, cultural exiles—both white and black—come together on a Caribbean island where they live out their lives in a neatly compartmentalized bourgeois fashion: the candy magnate Valerian Street[6] in his stereophonic-equipped greenhouse; his wife, cloistered in her bedroom; and the servants, Odine and Sydney, ensconced in their comfortable quarters. Daily life precludes "eruptions of funk," a lesson poignantly taught when Margaret Lenore discovers the bedraggled wild man, Son, in her closet. Although Son's appearance suggests Rastafarianism and outlawry, any shock value stirred by his discovery is canceled when he, too, proves to be just another exile. Except for one brief incident, when Odine kills a chicken and in plucking it recalls a moment from her distant past when she worked for a poultry butcher, there are no smells, tastes, or tactile experiences to summon up the past. Rather, there is a surfeit of foods whose only quality is the calories they contain.

In contrast with Morrison's earlier novels, the past in *Tar Baby* is never brought to metaphoric juxtaposition with the present.

Rather, it is held separate and bracketed by dream. When Valerian Street, sipping a brandy in his greenhouse, lapses into daydream, his recollection of the past, which in essence contrasts entrepreneurial capitalism to modern corporate capitalism, does not intrude on his present retirement. The past is past, and the significant historical transition evoked is perceived as inaccessible and natural.

The past is made more remote when it informs a nighttime dream. This is the case for Sydney, who every night dreams of his boyhood in Baltimore. "It was a tiny dream he had each night that he would never recollect from morning to morning. So he never knew what it was exactly that refreshed him."[7] For the black man hanging to the coattails of the white upper bourgeoisie, who thinks of himself as a "Philadelphia Negro" (TB, 61), the back streets of Baltimore are a social debit. His desire for assimilation to white bourgeois culture and the many years spent in service to the bourgeois class negate his ever experiencing the deep sensual and emotional pleasure that Pilate has whenever she beholds a blue sky or bites into a vine-ripened tomato.

With every dreamer dreaming a separate dream, there are no bridges to the past and no possibility of sharing an individual experience as part of a group's social history. Although a reminiscence like Pilate's recognition of the color blue can be communicated, a dream, as Son finds out, cannot be pressed into another dreamer's head. Son's dream of "yellow houses with white doors" and "fat black ladies in white dresses minding the pie table in the church" (TB, 119) is an image of wish fulfillment, rooted in private nostalgia. It bears no resemblance to his real past as we later come to understand it out of what the novel shows us of Eloe, Florida, where tough black women with little time for pie tables have built their own rough-hewn, unpainted homes.

For the "tar baby," Jadine, fashioned out of the rich white man's indulgence and the notions of culture most appealing to bourgeois America (European education and Paris "haute couture"), the past is irretrievable and no longer perceived as desirable. As the individual whose cultural exile is the most profound, Jadine is haunted by waking visions, born out of guilt and fear. In her most terrifying vision, a mob of black women—some familiar, some only known by their names—crowds into her room. Revealing, then waving, their breasts at her, they condemn Jadine for having abandoned the traditional maternal role of black women.

Whereas Jadine lives her separation from the past and rejection of traditional cultural roles with tormented uncertainty and frenzied activity, Milkman, in Morrison's previous novel, experiences his alienation from black culture as a hollow daily monotony. Jadine, whose desire to find self and be free leads to jet hops between Paris, the Caribbean, and New York, has not had the benefit of a powerful cultural mentor like Pilate, who awakens Milkman's desire to know his past. In contrast, all of Jadine's possible cultural heroes are bracketed by her rupture with the past and her class position. Jadine rejects family—her Aunt Odine, for her homey ways and maternal nature—and culture— the black islanders, so remote from Jadine's trajectory into the future that she never even bothers to learn their names.

Milkman, on the other hand, has been born and raised in the ghetto, albeit in the biggest house. He has never been to college, but he has had the benefit of teachers—both the street-wise Guitar and the folk-wise Pilate. If Milkman's present is a meaningless void of bourgeois alienation, the possibility of a past opens out to him like a great adventure. A quest for gold initiates Milkman's journey into the past—and into the self—but gold is not the novel's real object. Imagining that gold will free him from his father's domination and his family's emotional blackmail, Milkman comes to realize that only by knowing the past can he hope to have a future.

There is a sense of urgency in Morrison's writing, produced by the realization that a great deal is at stake. The novels may focus on individual characters like Milkman and Jadine, but the salvation of individuals is not the point. Rather, these individuals, struggling to reclaim or redefine themselves, are portrayed as epiphenomenal to community and culture, and it is the strength and continuity of the black cultural heritage as a whole that is at stake and being tested.

As Morrison sees it, the most serious threat to black culture is the obliterating influence of social change. The opening line from *Sula* might well have been the novel's conclusion, so complete is the destruction it records: "In that place, where they tore the night shade and blackberry patches from their roots to make room for the Medallion City Golf Course, there was once a neighborhood."[8] This is the community Morrison is writing to reclaim. Its history, terminated and dramatically obliterated, is condensed into a single sentence whose content spans from rural South to urban redevelopment. Here, as throughout Morrison's writing, natural imagery refers to the past, the rural South, the reservoir of culture that has been uprooted—like the blackberry bushes—to make way for modernization. In contrast, the future is perceived of as an amorphous, institutionalized power embodied in the notion of "Medallion City," which suggests neither nature nor a people. Joining the past to the future is the neighborhood, which occupies a very different temporal moment (which history has shown to be transitional), and defines a very different social mode, as distinct from its rural origins as it is from the amorphous urban future.

It is impossible to read Morrison's four novels without coming to see the neighborhood as a concept crucial to her understanding of history. The neighborhood defines a Northern social mode rather than a Southern one, for it describes the relationship of an economic satellite, contiguous to a larger metropolis rather than separate subsistence economics like the Southern rural towns of Shalimar and Eloe. It is a Midwestern phenomenon rather than a Northeastern big-city category, because it defines the birth of principally first-generation, Northern, working-class black communities. It is a mode of the forties rather than the sixties or the

eighties, and it evokes the many locally specific black populations in the North before these became assimilated to a larger,
more generalized, and less regionally specific sense of black culture that we today refer to as the "black community."

The fact that Milkman embarks on a quest for his past is itself
symptomatic of the difference between the forties neighborhood
and the sixties community. In contrast with Milkman, the black
youth of the forties had no need to uncover and decipher the past
simply because enough of it was still present, born on successive
waves of Southern black immigrants. For Milkman the past is a
riddle, a reality locked in the verses of a children's song (the
"song of Solomon") whose meaning is no longer explicit because
time has separated the words from their historical content.
Childhood and the way children perceive the world are again a
figure for a mode of existence prior to the advent of capitalism
and bourgeois society. And in *Song of Solomon*, it coincides with
the function of song in all marginal cultures as the unwritten
text of history and culture.

Milkman's quest is a journey through geographic space in
which the juxtaposition of the city and the countryside represents the relationship of the present to the past. In tracing his
roots from the Detroit ghetto, where he was familiar with Pilate's version of the Solomon song; to Danville, Pennsylvania,
where his father grew up; and then to Shalimar, Virginia, where
his grandfather was born and children still sing of Solomon,
Milkman deciphers the twin texts of history: song and genealogy. In so doing, he reconstructs a dialectic of historical transition, in which individual genealogy evokes the history of black
migration and the chain of economic expropriation from hinter-
land to village, and village to metropolis. The end point of Milkman's journey is the starting point of his race's history in this
country: slavery. The confrontation with the reality of slavery,
coming at the end of Milkman's penetration into historical process, is liberational because slavery is not portrayed as the origin
of history and culture. Instead, the novel opens out to Africa, the

source, and takes flight on the wings of Milkman's great-grandfather, the original Solomon. With the myth of the "flying Africans" (*SOS*, 332) Morrison transforms the moment of coming to grips with slavery as an allegory of liberation.

The fact that geographic space functions for history is symptomatic of a time when a people's past no longer forms a continuity with the present. It is one of the features that differentiates literary modernism from realism, in which people's lives are portrayed as integral to the flow of history. Because the past is perceived as problematical and historical transition is represented by the relationship among countryside, village, and city, *Song of Solomon* is very similar to the great modernist novels of the Latin American "Boom" (the literary movement born with the Cuban Revolution and brought to an end with the assassination of Allende). In Morrison's *Song of Solomon*, as in the Peruvian Mario Vargas Llosa's *La Casa Verde*, the synchronic relationship defined in geographic space stands for a diachronic relationship. The most interesting feature about these modernist texts is that, in reading them, the reader, like Milkman, restores diachrony to the text and, in so doing, realizes the historical dialectic that the text presents as inaccessible.

Milkman's journey into the past takes him out of consumer society, where he, Christmas shopping in the Rexall store, practices the translation of human emotions into commodities, and thrusts him into the preindustrial world of Shalimar, where for the first time in his life Milkman sees women with "nothing in their hands" (*SOS*, 262). Stunned, Milkman realizes that he "had never in his life seen a woman on the street without a purse slung over her shoulder, pressed under her arm, or dangling from her clenched fingers" (*SOS*, 262). The vision of women walking empty-handed produces an estrangement of Milkman's normal view of women who, conditioned by a market economy, haul around purses like grotesque bodily appendages.

The descent into the past means stepping out of reified and fetishized relationships. Milkman's sensitivities are abruptly awakened when, trudging through the woods, he is scratched by branches, bruised by rocks, and soaked in a stream. As all of his commodified possessions fall away—his watch, his Florsheim shoes, and his three-piece suit—he comes to realize a full range of sensual perceptions (along with some human social practices—like sharing) he had never before experienced. Entering Solomon's General Store, Milkman is struck by its dramatic antithesis to the big-city department store, in which money (rather than need or use) mediates the exchange of human identities for brand names.

For Macon Dead, Milkman's father, all human relationships have become fetishized by their being made equivalent to money. His wife is an acquisition; his son, an investment in the future; and his renters, dollar signs in the bank. The human sentiments he experienced as a boy have given way to the emotional blackmail he wages as an adult. Driven by the desire to own property, the basis of bourgeois class politics, Macon Dead uses property, like a true capitalist, for further accumulation through the collection of rents. When Milkman, echoing his father's words, refers to money as "legal tender," he reveals how deeply fetishized and abstracted the concept of money itself has become. In this context, the search for gold takes on new meaning as a search for the only unfetishized form of value and, in an allegorical sense, as the retrieval of unfetishized human relationships.

However, Macon Dead is not so totally integrated into the bourgeois class that he cannot sense the impoverishment of his life—"his wife's narrow unyielding back; his daughters, boiled dry from years of yearning; his son, to whom he could speak only if his words held some command or criticism" (SOS, 28–29). A phantom in search of some vision of human fulfillment, Macon wanders one evening into the southside ghetto, his sister's neighborhood. There, drawn by her singing, he pauses to peer in her window. In every way Pilate is her brother's emotional and social antithesis. What Macon sees when he looks into Pilate's house is a totally alternative life-style, whose dramatic opposition to the spiritual impoverishment of Macon's world gives rise to a utopian moment:

> . . . he crept up to the side window where the candlelight flickered lowest, and peeped in. Reba was cutting her toenails with a kitchen knife or a switchblade, her long neck bent almost to her knees. The girl, Hagar, was braiding her hair, while Pilate, whose face he could not see because her back was to the window, was stirring something in a pot. Wine pulp, perhaps. Macon knew it was not food she was stirring, for she and her daughters ate like children. Whatever they had a taste for. No meal was ever planned or balanced or served. Nor was there any gathering at the table. Pilate might bake hot bread and each one of them would eat it with butter whenever she felt like it. Or there might be grapes, left over from the winemaking, or peaches for days on end. If one of them bought a gallon of milk they drank it until it was gone. If another got a half bushel of tomatoes or a dozen ears of corn, they ate them until they were gone too. They ate what they had or came across or had a craving for. Profits from their wine-selling evaporated like sea water in a hot wind—going for junk jewelry for Hagar, Reba's gifts to men, and he didn't know what all. (SOS, 29)

In its journey back to rural origins, the novel demonstrates that Pilate's household is not, as this passage tends to suggest, structured in infantile desires and relationships, but that the world of childhood is rooted in rural society, where reciprocity and the unmediated response to desire determine social life. The utopian aspect of Pilate's household is not contained within it, but generated out of its abrupt juxtaposition to the bourgeois mode of her brother's household. In contrast to Macon's world, which is based on accumulation, Pilate's household is devoted in true potlatch fashion to nonaccumulation. With everyone working to separate berries from thorns, winemaking is not a means for creating surplus value, but a communal social activity whose natural raw material suggests, in Morrison's symbolic register, another link to rural agricultural society. Reba, who wins lotteries and department-store giveaways, enjoys a noncommodified relationship to objects, in which value is defined not by an object's monetary equivalent but by the spontaneous way she comes to possess it and the pleasure it renders in the giving. Finally, Pilate's only pretense to property ownership is purely symbolic: a bag of bones, which turn out to be her father's, and rocks, a single one gathered from every state she has visited.

Throughout her writing Morrison defines and tests the limits of individual freedom. Unlike those characters who realize total freedom and, as a result, are incapable of living in society and maintaining human relationships, like Cholly Breedlove[9] and Sula, Pilate lives an unencumbered life that is the basis for a social form of freedom, rich in human understanding and love, which is neither sexual nor familial. In the text, Pilate's freedom, which makes her different from everybody else, has a very curious explanation: namely, the lack of a navel.

Now, it would be wrong simply to see Pilate's lack as just one more example of the mutilated, deformed, and stigmatized characters who tend to crop up in Morrison's writing. And it would be equally wrong to dismiss these forms of physical difference as nothing more than the author's obsession with freaks of nature. Rather, as Morrison herself indicates, Pilate's lack is to be read in social terms. The lack of a navel, like the other versions of physical deformity, functions as a metaphor that allows the reader to perceive a unique personal relationship to society as a whole.

Born without a navel, Pilate is a product of an unnatural birth. In social terms, her father dead and having never known her mother, she is an orphan. Her smooth, unbroken abdominal skin causes her to be shunned by everyone who either befriends her or comes to be her lover. Consequently, she has "no people." Because no clan claims her, she is outside all the potentially limiting aspects of blood relationships and traditional forms of social behavior. Apparently without a past and a place, Pilate embodies the "mythic hero"[10] first portrayed by Faulkner's Thomas Sutpen in *Absalom! Absalom!* The difference between Faulkner and Morrison, conditioned by the intervening years, which have brought black civil rights, countercultural politics, and the feminist perspective, is that, while Morrison invests her "mythic hero" with utopian aspirations, Faulkner does not. In making Sutpen and his "design" for plantation and progeny the epitome of Southern class society, Faulkner negates the utopian potential that his mythic outsider first represents in opposition to the stifled, small-town sensibilities of Jefferson, Mississippi.

Another dimension that Pilate's lack of a navel allows the reader to experience is the child's discovery of sexual difference. The metaphor of lack articulates the relationship between the advent of adult sexuality and the way it transforms the individual's relationship to others. As a child, having seen only her brother's and father's stomachs, Pilate imagines that navels, like penises, are something men have and women lack. Later, when others point to her lack as a form of freakishness, Pilate achieves adult sexuality only to have it denied her. Deprived of sex because of her unique body and the superstitious fear it creates, Pilate's lack becomes the basis for her liberation from narrowly defined human relationships based on sexuality and the expansion of her social world to one based on human sensitivity. This is very different from the way Pilate's sister-in-law, Ruth Foster, lives her sexual deprivation. Shunned by her husband, she turns inward to necrophiliac fantasies of her father, a mildly obscene relationship with her son, and masturbation. Ruth, like many of Morrison's female characters, is dependent on a possessive and closed heterosexual relationship; she never comes to see human relationships as anything but sexual. For her, the denial of sex simply means a more narrowly defined sexuality and the closure of her social world.

The only aspect of Pilate's lack as a metaphor for social relationships that is not explicit but does, nevertheless, inform

Morrison's treatment of Pilate is its function as a figure for the experience of racial otherness. This is not the case for other instances of lack, which, like Pecola's lack of blue eyes and Hagar's lack of copper-colored hair, capture the horror of seeing oneself as "other" and inferior. Although Pilate, like many of Morrison's other characters, does undergo a moment of looking at (and into) the self, during which she recognizes her lack (or difference) and, as a consequence, determines to live her life according to a very different set of values, her moment of self-recognition (unlike many of theirs) is not couched in racial terms. Because lack in every other instance is a figure for the experience of race, it would seem to be implicit—if not explicit—in the characterization of Pilate. There is just no need for Pilate to affirm herself through race as the shell-shocked Shadrack does in *Sula* when, amnesiac and terrified by his own body, he glimpses the reflection of his face and sees in it the bold reality of his "unequivocal" blackness. For Pilate, blackness is already unequivocal. And pastlessness does not endanger identity, or separate her from society, as it does for Shadrack. Rather, it liberates the self into society.

As a literary figure for examining the lived experience of social difference, and testing the human potential for liberation, lack has its opposite in a full term: bodily stigma. In contrast to Pilate, who has no mark, Sula possesses a striking birthmark above her eye. A patch of skin unlike that found on any other human, Sula's birthmark is thought to represent a tadpole, a flower, or a snake depending on the mood of the beholder. Stigma is the figural equivalent of Sula's role in the community. As a social pariah branded as different, she is the freedom against which others define themselves.

Bodily deformity is another metaphor for the experience of social difference. When Shadrack awakes in a hospital bed, he comes into a world so totally fragmented and sundered that he is unsure where his own hands might be; after all, "anything could be anywhere" (S, 8). When he finally does behold his hands, he imagines that they are monstrously deformed—so terrifyingly that he cannot bear to look at them. Totally disoriented, his hands hidden behind his back, Shadrack is expelled from the hospital and pushed out into the world—a lone, cringing figure in an alien landscape.

For Morrison, the psychological, like the sensual and sexual, is also historical. In a novel whose opening describes the leveling of a neighborhood and its transformation into the Medallion City Golf Course, Shadrack's experience of bodily fragmentation is the psychological equivalent of annihilating social upheaval, which he was subjected to as an army draftee (the army being the first of capitalism's modern industrial machines to incorporate black men). Shadrack's imagined physical deformity is a figure for the equally monstrous psychological and social transformations that capitalism in all its modes (slavery, the military, and wage labor) has inflicted on the minds and bodies of black people.

Shadrack's affirmation of self, arising out of the moment he sees his image reflected in a toilet bowl and beholds the solid and profound reality of his blackness, ranks as one of the most powerful literary statements of racial affirmation. Race is the wellspring of Shadrack's inalienable identity. Everything around him and within him may be subject to transformation, but his blackness is forever. This sense of continuity in the face of chaos lies at the heart of Shadrack's cryptic, one-word message to the child Sula: " 'Always' " (S, 53). It is the basis for both Shadrack's and Sula's reinsertion into society as representations of freedom. As both messiah and pariah, Shadrack is marginal, accepted by, but never assimilated into, the black community. He, like Sula and Morrison's other social pariah, Soaphead Church, provides a point of perspective on the community that is both interior and exterior; he allows the community to define itself against a form of freedom, which being a social unit, it cannot attain. Morrison's characters demonstrate that the black community tolerates difference, whereas the white bourgeois world shuts difference out. She underscores the fact that for the white world, under capitalism, difference, because it articulates a form of freedom, is a threat and therefore must be institutionalized or jailed.

In *Tar Baby*, bodily deformity takes a very different form. Because this novel describes an already-sundered black community whose exiles have neither the wish nor the capacity to rediscover the source of black culture, freedom cannot be articulated (as it was in the previous novels) by an individual's moment of self-affirmation and reinsertion into society. Having no possible embodiment in the real world—not even as a pariah—freedom takes mythic form and defines the text's alternate, subterranean world, in which, in sharp contrast with the bourgeois world of manor house and leisure, a centuries-old band of blind black horsemen rides the swamps.

Blindness is another way of giving metaphoric expression to social difference and freedom.[11] It overlaps with the function of lack in that the lack of sight, which in bourgeois society is the basis for an individual's alienation, is in the mythic world the basis for the group's cohesion and absolute alternality. This is because blindness is not portrayed as an individual's affliction, but rather a communally shared way of being in the world. Once again, the figure of deformity evokes a historical reality. The myth of the blind horsemen has its roots in the many real maroon societies whose very existence depended on seclusion and invisibility. This is the social reality for which blindness is a metaphoric reversal.

A final metaphor for social otherness is self-mutilation.[12] Unlike lack and deformity, self-mutilation represents the individual's direct confrontation with the oppressive social forces inherent in white domination. Because it functions as a literary figure, self-mutilation is portrayed in Morrison's writing as liberational and contrasts sharply with all the other forms of violence done to the self. For instance, when Polly Breedlove lashes out at her child Pecola, berating her and beating her for spilling a berry cobbler while at the same time comforting and cuddling the white child in her charge, she internalizes her hate for white society and deflects the spontaneous eruption of violence away from its real object and toward a piece of herself. Unlike Polly Breedlove's violence toward the self, which locks her in profound self-hatred, self-mutilation is portrayed as a confrontational tactic that catapults the individual out of an oppressive situation. Because it involves severing a part of the body, self-mutilation coincides with the figure of lack and intensifies (by reason of direct articulation) the potential for expressing freedom. In Morrison's writing, self-mutilation brings about the spontaneous redefinition of the individual, not as an alienated cripple—as would be the case in bourgeois society—but as a new and whole person, occupying a radically different social space.

When, as an adolescent, Sula is confronted by a band of teenage Irish bullies, she draws a knife. Instead of threatening the boys with it or plunging it into one of them, she whacks off the tip of her own finger. Terrified, the boys run away. Sula's self-mutilation symbolizes castration and directly contests the white male sexual domination of black women that the taunting and threatening boys evoke. Her act, coupled with words of warning, " 'If I can do that to myself, what you suppose I'll do to you?' " (S, 54), represents the refusal—no matter how high the cost—to accept and cower in the face of domination.

For its defiance of oppressive social norms as well as its symbolic nature, Sula's act of self-mutilation has its precedent in her grandmother's solution to a similar confrontation with bourgeois-dominated society. Abandoned by her husband, with three small children and nothing but five eggs and three beets among them, Eva Peace takes a truly radical course of action that lifts her out of the expected role of an abandoned black mother circa 1921, who could do no more than live hand-to-mouth, and gives her a very different future. Leaving her children in the care of a neighbor, she sets out. "Eighteen months later she swept down from a wagon with two crutches, a new black pocketbook,

and one leg" (*S*, 34). Eva never confirms neighborhood specula-
tion that she allowed a train to sever her leg because the way in
which she lost it is not important. The real issue is what her self-
mutilation enables her to achieve. As the juxtaposition between
Eva's "new black pocketbook" and "one leg" suggests, monthly
insurance checks make it possible for her to build a new life. The
construction of a rambling, many-roomed house for family and
boarders gives physical evidence of Eva's confrontation with and
manipulation of the written laws of white society, whose unwritten laws would have condemned her to a life of poverty.

Yet the most radical aspect of Eva's act is not the simple and
direct contestation of capitalism that her self-mutilation represents but the subsequent lack that allows a wholly new social
collective to come into being around her. If the loss of a limb
means that Eva practically never leaves her room, it does not signify withdrawal. Instead, Eva is "sovereign" of an entire household, which includes three generations of Peace women as its
nucleus (Eva, Hannah, and Sula); their boarders (the young married couples and an alcoholic hillbilly); and their adopted out-
casts (the three Deweys). For its fluid composition, openness to
outsiders, and organization on a feminine principle, Eva's household represents a radical alternative to the bourgeois family
model.

At one level, Morrison writes to awaken her reader's sensitivity, to shake up and disrupt the sensual numbing that accompanies social and psychological alienation. This is the function of
her "eruptions of funk," which include metaphors drawn from
past moments of sensual fulfillment as well as the use of lack,
deformity, and self-mutilation as figures for liberation. At a
deeper level, and as a consequence of these features, Morrison's
writing often allows an alternative social world to come into being. When this happens, "otherness" no longer functions as an
extension of domination (as it does when blackness is beheld
from the point of view of racist bourgeois society, or when the
crippled, blind, and deformed are compared to the terrorizing to-

tality of a whole and therefore "perfect" body). Rather, the space created by otherness permits a reversal of domination and transforms what was once perceived from without as "other" into the explosive image of a utopian mode. Morrison's most radical "eruption of funk" is the vision of an alternative social world. It comes into view when Macon Dead peers into Pilate's window; when the child Nel, the product of her mother's stifled bourgeois morality, scratches at Sula's screen door; and when the intimidated and fearful Pecola visits her upstairs neighbors, the three prostitutes.

It is not gratuitous that in all these cases the definition of social utopia is based on a three-woman household. This does not imply a lesbian orientation, because in all cases the women are decidedly heterosexual. Rather, these are societies that do not permit heterosexuality as it articulates male domination to be the determining principle for the living and working relationships of the group, as it is in capitalist society.

Morrison's three-woman utopian households contrast dramatically with an earlier literary version that occurs, paradoxically again, in Faulkner's *Absalom! Absalom!*. During the grinding culmination of the Civil War, the men all gone—siphoned off by the army, the economy reduced to bare subsistence, the novel brings together three women: Judith, Sutpen's daughter and heir; Clytie, Sutpen's black nonheir; and the young spinstress, Miss Rosa, Sutpen's nonbetrothed. Taking refuge in the shell of a once-prosperous manor house, they eke out their survival on a day-to-day basis:

> So we waited for him. We led the busy eventless lives of three nuns in a barren and poverty-stricken convent: the walls we had were safe, impervious enough, even if it did not matter to the walls whether we ate or not. And amicably, not as two white women and a negress, not as three negroes or three whites, not even as three women, but merely as three creatures who still possessed the need to eat but took no pleasure in it, the need to sleep but from it no joy

in weariness or regeneration, and in whom sex was some
forgotten atrophy like the rudimentary gills we call the ton-
sils or the still-opposable thumbs for old climbing.[13]

In considering the cataclysm of the Civil War and its destruction
of traditional Southern society, Faulkner is led to imagine the basis for a potentially radical new form of social organization,
based on subsistence rather than accumulation and women
rather than men. However, the incipient possibility of social utopia dies stillborn, because the male principle and the system of
patrimony have not been transformed or refuted, but merely displaced. Sutpen, even in his absence, is still the center of the
household. Race, too, is not confronted or transcended. Rather,
it, like sex, is simply dismissed. And with it go all vestiges of humanity.

The tremendous differences between Faulkner and Morrison,
which include historical period, race, and sex, lie at the heart of
their dramatically opposed images: the one dystopian; the other
utopian. Rather than dwell on the social and historical factors
that shape their fiction, I will emphasize the ways in which historical differences are manifested in the texts. Faulkner's dehumanized monads and the routinized lives they lead contrast
sharply with Morrison's portrayal of Pilate's household, in which
individual differences between the three women function to test
the social dynamic within the group, and between it and society
at large. Faulkner's retrenched espousal of the male-dominated
social model and his tenacious refusal to imagine anything else
condition his bleak vision of society. On the other hand, Morrison's projection of a social utopia arises from its confrontation
with and reversal of the male-dominated bourgeois social model.
Rather than systematically leveling social problems, Morrison
foregrounds them. The utopian aspect of her vision is produced
by the totality of its opposition to society at large—not by its individual members. This makes her portrayal very different from
classical literary utopias, whose individuals are presented as per-

fect and harmonious models. None of Morrison's individual characters in any of her three utopias is perfect. Rather than supplying answers to social problems, they give rise to questions about social relationships and society as a whole. Thus, Pilate demonstrates the insufficiency of the agrarian social mode to provide for its members once they are transplanted to urban consumer society. Her strength and resourcefulness cannot be passed on to her daughter and granddaughter because each is more distant from the rural society in which Pilate worked and grew up. Their experience of insufficiency leads to hollow consumption (Reba's of sex and Hagar's of commodities) and demonstrates the way consumer society penetrates and impoverishes human relationships.

When in *Tar Baby* "funk" erupts as myth, its potential for estranging fetishized relationships is minimized because of its distance from the urban and suburban settings that condition the lives of more and more Americans, both black and white. Son's quest for the mythic community of blind maroon horsemen that ends *Tar Baby* may represent a dramatic departure from his previous endeavors, but it does not bring disruption into the heart of social practice, as occurs when the image of Pilate's household bursts upon Macon Dead's alienated and numbed sensibilities. Although *Song of Solomon* also has a mythic dimension, myth is not the novel's only form of "funk." Then, too, myth is integral to Milkman's concrete past, as he discovers by following his family's route back to slavery, whereas for Son, it represents a very distant cultural source not directly linked to his present.

"Funk" is really nothing more than the intrusion of the past into the present. It is most oppositional when it juxtaposes a not-so-distant social mode to those evolved under bourgeois society. Morrison's method might be thought of as a North American variant of the magical realism that we have come to associate with Gabriel García Marquez. If in his *One Hundred Years of Solitude* pleasurable delight is synonymous with barbed political criticism, this is because the text's metaphoric incidents and characters are created out of the juxtaposition of First and Third World realities. Just as domination and dependency create separation and inequality between North and South America, so too do Marquez's metaphors represent the unresolved contradiction between two possible readings: the one mythic and pleasurable, the other historical and critical. The same holds true for Morrison, only the terms of her geographic and historical equation are bound up and framed by the history of the United States. North/South, black/white, these are the ingredients of Morrison's magical realism whose tension-fraught and unresolved juxtapositions articulate the continuation of domination in our society and the persistence of racism, and at the same time provoke Morrison's creative and critical imagination.

5. Alice Walker's Women

Be nobody's darling
Be an outcast.
Take the contradictions
Of your life
And wrap around
You like a shawl,
To parry stones
To keep you warm.[1]

What the black Southern writer
inherits as a natural right is
a sense of community.[2]

The strength of Alice Walker's writing derives from the author's inexorable recognition of her place in history; the sensitivity of her work, from her profound sense of community; its beauty, from her commitment to the future. Many readers associate Alice Walker with her most recent novel, *The Color Purple*, for which she won a Pulitzer Prize. But the best place to begin to define the whole of her writing is with the semiautobiographical novel, *Meridian*. In that novel I suggest we first consider a very minor character: "Wile Chile." For "Wile Chile" is not gratuitous, not an aberrant whim on the part of the author, but an epigramatic representation of all the women Walker brings to life. I think this is how Walker intended it, precisely because she begins telling about Meridian by describing her confrontation with "Wile Chile," a thirteen-year-old ghetto urchin, who from the age of about five or six, when she was first spotted, has fed and clothed herself out of garbage cans. More slippery than a "greased pig" and as wary as any stray, the Wild Child is virtually uncatchable. When it becomes obvious that the Wild Child is pregnant, Meridian takes it upon herself to bring her into the fold. Baiting her with glass beads and cigarettes, she eventually catches "Wile Chile," leads her back to the campus, bathes and feeds her, then sets about finding a home for her. However, Meridian's role as mother comes to an abrupt end when "Wile Chile" escapes and bolts into the street where she is struck by a speeding car.

If we consider the story of "Wile Chile" against the events that shape Meridian's development from childhood (the daughter of schoolteachers), through college, into the Civil Rights movement and finally to embark on her own more radical commitment to revolutionary praxis, the two pages devoted to the Wild Child seem at most a colorful digression. Her only language comprised of obscenities and farts, "Wile Chile" is Meridian's social antithesis. Nevertheless, the story of "Wile Chile" is central to our understanding of *Meridian* and the woman whose name is the title of this book, for it includes certain basic features, present in different forms in all the anecdotal incidents that make up the novel and through which Meridian herself must struggle in the process of her self-affirmation.

When Meridian drags the stomach-heavy "Wile Chile" back to her room, she puts herself in the role of mother and enacts a mode of mothering that smacks of liberal bourgeois sentimentality. On the other hand, "Wile Chile"'s own impending motherhood represents absolute abandonment to biological contingency. These are only two of the many versions of womanhood that the problem of mothering will provoke in the book. Although Meridian and "Wile Chile" do not share a common social ground, they come together on one point, and that is the possibility of being made pregnant. For "Wile Chile" and Meridian both, conception articulates oppression, to which "Wile Chile" succumbs and against which Meridian struggles to discover whether it is possible for a black woman to emerge as a self and at the same time fulfill the burdens of motherhood.

The story of "Wile Chile" also raises the question of Meridian's relationship to the academic institution and the black community that surrounds the university. Her outrageous behavior causes Meridian (and the reader) to reflect on the function of the university as a social institution whose primary role is to assimilate bright young black women, who might otherwise be dangerously marginal, to a dominant white culture. "Wile Chile" 's unpermissible language draws attention to the tremendous pressures also placed on Meridian to become a "lady" patterned after white European cultural norms. This is not a cosmetic transformation, but one that separates the individual from her class and community and forever inscribes her within the bourgeois world. That the university serves bourgeois class interests is dramatized when Saxon College students and members of the local black community attempt to hold "Wile Chile" 's funeral on the campus. Barred from entering the university, the funeral procession is isolated and defined as "other" in the same way that the local neighborhood, which ought to be the university's community of concern, is instead its ghetto.

In *Meridian*, childbearing is consistently linked to images of murder and suicide. In this, the figure of the Wild Child is as much a paradigm for the book's main characters, Meridian and Lynne, as it is for another minor anecdotal figure, Fast Mary. As the students at Saxon College tell it, Fast Mary secretly gave birth in a tower room, chopped her newborn babe to bits, and washed it down the toilet. When her attempt to conceal the birth fails, her parents lock her up in a room without windows where Fast Mary subsequently hangs herself. In posing the contradictory social constraints that demand simultaneously that a woman be both a virgin and sexually active, the parable of Fast Mary prefigures the emotional tension Meridian herself will experience as a mother, expressing it in fantasies of murder and suicide. The tales of "Wile Chile" and Fast Mary also pose the problem of the individual's relationship to the group. Fast Mary's inability to call on her sister students and her final definitive isolation at the hands of her parents raise questions Meridian will also confront: is there a community of support? And is communication possible between such a community and the individual who is seen as a social iconoclast?

The problem of communication, and specifically the question of language, is at the heart of another of *Meridian's* anecdotal characters: Louvinie, a slave woman from West Africa whose parents excelled in a particular form of storytelling, one designed to ensnare anyone guilty of having committed a crime. Louvinie's duties as a slave are to cook and mind the master's children. The latter includes her own superb mastery of the art of storytelling, which for Louvinie, as for all oppressed peoples, functions to keep traditional culture alive and to provide a context for radical social practice. The radical potential of language is abundantly clear when the master's weakhearted young son dies of heart failure in the middle of one of Louvinie's gruesome tales.

At the level of overt content, the story of Louvinie focuses on the function of language; in its structure, it reproduces the features associated in the book with motherhood. Louvinie, who does not have children of her own, nevertheless functions as a mother to the master's offspring. She, like "Wile Chile," Fast Mary, even Meridian and Lynne, kills the child defined structurally as her own. In more narrow terms, Louvinie provides a model closer to the way Meridian will resolve her life. Her actual childlessness suggests in asexual terms Meridian's choice not to be fertile and bear children. Moreover, when Louvinie murders the child in her charge it is clearly a politically contestatory act, which is not the case for either "Wile Chile" or Fast Mary—but is true for Meridian when she chooses to abort her child.

Louvinie's punishment rejoins the problem of language, as the master cuts out her tongue. Louvinie's response is to bury her tongue under a small magnolia tree, which, generations later, grows to be the largest magnolia in the country and stands at the center of Saxon College. As a natural metaphor, the tree is in opposition to the two social institutions—the plantation and the university—and suggests an alternative to their definition of black history and language. Just as the university excludes women like "Wile Chile," so too does it seek to silence black folk culture typified by Louvinie's stories. The magnolia casts the university in stark relief, exposes its version of history as a lie, its use of language as collaborative with the forces of domination.

The magnolia also provides a figural bridge linking the struggle of black women from slavery to the present. In the past, it offered a hiding place for escaped slaves and in the present its enormous trunk and branches provide a platform for classes. Named The Sojourner, the magnolia conjures up the presence of another leader of black women, who, like Louvinie, used language in the struggle for liberation. In this way, Walker builds a network of women, some mythic like Louvinie, some real like Sojourner Truth, as the context for Meridian's affirmation and radicalization.

As the stories of "Wile Chile" and Fast Mary demonstrate, anecdotes are the basic narrative units in Walker's fiction. They reveal how Walker has managed to keep the storytelling tradition among black people alive in the era of the written narrative. The anecdotes are pedagogical. They allow the reader to experience the same structural features, recast with each telling, in a different historical and social setting. Each telling demands that the college students (and the reader) examine and define their relationship to the group in a more profound way than in the explicitly political gatherings where each is asked to state what she will do for the revolution. In this way, Walker defines story writing in the radical tradition that storytelling has had among black people.

It is not surprising that language is crucial to Meridian's process of becoming. From slavery to the present, black women have spoken out against their oppression, and when possible, written their version of history. However, their narratives have fared less well in the hands of publishers and the reading public than those written by black men. Only very recently and with the growing interest in writers like Morrison, Marshall, and Walker have black women enjoyed better access to recognized channels of communication outside those of home and church. As testament to the very long struggle for recognition waged by black women and the deep oppression out of which their struggle began, the literature is full of characters like Hurston's Janie Woods, whose husband sees and uses her like a "mule" and will not allow her to speak, to Walker's most recent female character, Celie, in *The Color Purple*, also denied a voice, who out of desperation for meaningful dialogue writes letters to God. For black women writers, the problem of finding a viable literary language—outside of the male canon defined predominantly by Richard Wright—has generated a variety of literary strategies. Morrison's solution was to develop a highly metaphorical language,[3] whereas for Walker the solution has been the anecdotal narrative, which because of its relationship to storytelling and the family more closely approximates a woman's linguistic practice than does Morrison's very stylized discourse.

The fact is no black woman has ever been without language, not even the tongueless Louvinie, who uses the magical preparation and planting of her tongue to speak louder and longer than words. The question of language is not meaningful except in relation to the community. Louvinie's example affirms that the community of struggle will always exist and that the actions of a single black woman join the network of all. In contrast, "Wile Chile" represents a negation of the individual's need for community. With language reduced to farts and swears, hers is a one-way communication whose every enunciation denies integration with the group and proclaims her absolute marginality. Contrary to the Wild Child's self-destructive marginality, Meridian must define a form of oneness with herself that will allow her to speak and work with the community and at the same time will prevent becoming submerged by it. Meridian's quest for a language and a praxis is analogous to Walker's work as a writer, which demands both distance from and integration with the people.

When, in the book's first chapter, Meridian is asked if she could kill for the revolution, she finds herself unable to make the required revolutionary affirmation and defines instead what will be her more difficult form of revolutionary praxis: "I'll go back to the people."[4] People means the South, the small towns, the communities for whom the Civil Rights movement passed by too quickly to transform embedded racist and sexist practices. In this, she is the antithesis of "Wile Chile," who never was a part of any community and hence can never return to one.

Meridian's decision is her way of defining the single most common feature in fiction by black women writers: that of return to the community. From Zora Neale Hurston's *Their Eyes Were Watching God*, to the recent novels by Toni Morrison, the trajectory of departure and return is the common means for describing a woman's development and structuring the novel. In every instance, return raises the fundamental question of whether a community of support exists and what will be the individual's relationship to it.

For Morrison's Sula, return articulates the tragic plight of an extremely sensitive and perceptive black woman, in many ways ahead of her time, who goes to college, sees the world and a fair number of men, only to find herself dispossessed of place. Although the community of her girlhood has undergone economic progress, neither the town's new golf course nor its convalescent hospital testify to deep social transformation. Sula returns home to find her girlhood friend deeply stigmatized by male sexual domination. Traumatized by his abandonment, she has become a sterile shell living out a life whose only excuse is her moral and economic enslavement to her children. There is no community of possibility for Sula, who dies alone with her dreams and aspirations—a halcyon symbol of a future womanhood that can never be the basis for a community in this society.

Walker's rendering of return involves elements present in both Hurston's tale of Janie Woods and Morrison's account of Sula, but set in an entirely different context: the Civil Rights movement, which historically was not a factor for Hurston and geographically does not significantly enter into Morrison's tales, which are usually set in the Midwest. Only in Walker, a writer of the Southern black experience, do we come to understand how psychically important the Civil Rights movement was—not that it solved anything, but it definitely marks the moment after which nothing can ever be the same. Meridian's mission is to help discover the shape of the future.

Return is the developmental imperative in all Walker's novels, where the journey over geographic space is a metaphor for personal growth and, in a larger sense, historical transformation. In her first novel, *The Third Life of Grange Copeland*, Walker's conception of geographic space embodies a dialectical understanding of history. When Grange Copeland abandons wife and child to seek self and fortune in New York City, he leaves behind a rural community historically representative of the plantation system for the North and the industrial mode. The third moment of the dialectic is marked by Grange's return to the South, not as a penniless sharecropper, but with money in his pocket to buy his own land. The farm Grange brings into being suggests Walker's vision of a very different basis for black community, one that has experienced and transcended two forms of enslavement: first to the plantation, then to wage labor. In Walker's vision of the fu-

ture, property ownership will not be for the purpose of accumulation as it is under capitalism, but will provide for the satisfaction of basic human material and spiritual needs.

The epic of Grange Copeland is doubly transformational in
that the character who will bear his experience into the future
(both of the distant past that Grange passes along in the form of
folktales and of the more recent past that Grange has directly
known) is not a male heir, as more traditional literature might
have it, but his granddaughter, whose coming-of-age is marked
by sit-ins, voter registration, and the speeches of Martin Luther
King, Jr. His own life marred by his struggle against bigotry, his
own acts of violence, and the terrible racism and sexism of
which he has been both a victim and an agent, Grange cannot be
the embodiment of the future. Rather, some great moment of
rupture from the past is needed, and this Walker achieves in the
transition from the male to the female principle. The novel ends
on a note of affirmation—but not without uncertainty over the
shape of the future. Ruth, Grange's granddaughter, is an adolescent and her future as well as the post–Civil Rights black community in the South cannot yet be told, but is, like the sixteen-
year-old Ruth, on the threshold of its becoming.[5]

In geographic strokes less broad, Walker's most recent novel,
The Color Purple, also articulates personal and historical transition. In it, Celie is married as an adolescent to a man who makes
her cook and keep house, tend the fields and look after his un-
ruly children from a previous marriage, and who pretty much
conceives of her as a "mule." Celie's abuse is deepened by the
fact that before marriage she had already been repeatedly raped
by the man she calls "father" and made to bear his children only
to have them taken from her soon after birth. If there is to be any
transformation in this book, its starting point is the absolute
rock bottom of a woman's economic and sexual enslavement in a
male-dominated and racist society.

The possibility of Celie's transformation is brought about by
her journey away from the rural backwater and to the big city,

Memphis, where she comes to support herself—not by means of wage labor (it is clear that Walker sees no hope for liberation in the transition to the industrial mode)—by means of learning a trade that is both artistic and necessary. She designs and sews custom pants.

If Celie's transformation is to be thorough, it must be not just economic, but sexual as well. Celie's ability to question what would otherwise be her "lot in life" and to break with her passive acceptance of her husband's domination is made possible by her friendship and eventual lesbian relationship with a black blues singer, Shug Avery. Unlike the monstrous inequality between husband and wife, theirs is a reciprocal relationship— Celie giving of herself to heal the sick and exhausted Shug (even though Celie's husband has for years been enamored of the singer), and Shug giving of herself, patiently and lovingly teaching Celie to know the joys of her own body and to follow the intuition of her mind. Neither the economics of pants-making nor the sexuality of lesbianism represents modes of enslavement as do the economics of industrial capitalism and the sexuality of male-dominated heterosexual relationships. At book's end Celie is neither seen as a pantsmaker in the way one might see an autoworker as a particular species of human, nor as a lesbian lover the way one sees a wife and mother.

Out of Walker's three novels, *The Color Purple* defines return in the most auspicious terms and offers not a prescription for but a suggestion of what a nonsexist, nonracist community might be. No longer a voiceless chattel to her man, Celie is able to converse with her husband. Having undergone liberation in both economic and sexual terms, she is for the first time perceived not as a domestic slave or the means toward male sexual gratification but as a whole woman: witty, resourceful, caring, wise, sensitive, and sensual. And her home—the site of an open and extended family where family and friends merge—suggests the basis for a wholly new community. The Fourth of July picnic that concludes the book and reunites Celie with her sister and children redefines the traditional family group in the context of a radically transformed household.

Of all of Walker's novels, *Meridian* offers the clearest view of the process of radicalization. For Meridian, the autobiographical embodiment of Walker herself, coming of age in the sixties does not offer a free ticket, but provides an atmosphere of confrontation and the questioning of contradiction with which the individual must grapple. Early in the book it becomes clear that one of the most profound ideologies to be confronted and transcended is the acceptance of mystical explanations for political realities. Meridian's childhood is steeped in Indian lore, the walls of her room papered with photographs of the great Indian leaders from Sitting Bull and Crazy Horse to the romanticized Hiawatha. Moreover, her father's farm includes an ancient Indian burial mound, its crest shaped like a serpent, where, in the coil of its tail, Meridian achieves a state of "ecstasy" (*M*, 53). Absorbed in a dizzying spin, she feels herself lifted out of her body while all around her—family and countryside—are caught up in the spinning whirlpool of her consciousness. It is not odd that Walker focuses on mystical experience. After all, this is a book about the sixties whose counterculture opened the door to more than one form of mysticism. It is also not strange that Meridian's mystical experience derives from Native American culture, given the long cohistorical relationship between blacks and Indians in the southeastern United States (their radical union goes back to the time of cimarrons and Seminoles).

However, ecstacy is not the answer. Although Meridian will learn from the mystical experience, it will not be sufficient to her life's work to rely on the practice of retreat into the ecstatic trance. What, then, of the historic link between Indians and blacks? If, in the course of the book, Meridian learns to transcend ecstasy, is this a denial of her (and her people's) relationship to the Indian people?

Definitely not. The book's epigraph gives another way of defining Meridian's relationship to Native Americans, which the great lesson taught by her radicalization will bring into reality. Taken from *Black Elk Speaks*, this is the epigraph:

> I did not know then how much was ended. When I look back now . . . I can still see the butchered women and children lying heaped and scattered all along the crooked gulch as plain as when I saw them with eyes still young. And I can see that something else died there in the bloody mud, and was buried in the blizzard. A people's dream died there. It was a beautiful dream . . . the nation's hoop is broken and scattered. There is no center any longer, and the sacred tree is dead.

Black Elk's words remember the massacre of Wounded Knee, which for Indian people was the brutal cancellation of their way of life. The dream Black Elk refers to is the vision he, as a holy man, had of his people and their world: "The leaves on the trees, the grasses on the hills and in the valleys, the waters in the creeks and in the rivers and the lakes, the four-legged and the two-legged and the wings of the air—all danced together to the music of the stallion's song."[6]

This is a vision of a community of man and nature, which Black Elk, as a holy man, must bring into being—not individually, but through the collective practice of the group. As he sees it, the nation is a "hoop" and "Everything an Indian does is in a circle, and that is because the Power of the World always works in circles, and everything tries to be round." These are images of a community's wholeness, which Meridian takes as her political paradigm—not the particulars of Indian culture; not the beads that hippies grafted on their white middle-class identities, not the swoons of ecstasy—but the Indian view of community, in which the holy man or seer is not marginal, but integral to the group. So when Meridian says she will "go back to the people" and when she leads them in demonstration against racist practices, she enacts Black Elk's formula for praxis. As an intellectual and a political activist, she understands that the individual's inspiration for social change can only be realized through the group's collective activity.

By far the greatest test of Meridian's radicalization is to overcome the social and sexual categories ascribed to all women, and black women in particular. Because she does not choose the lesbian alternative as Celie does in *The Color Purple,* Meridian's struggle is within and against heterosexual relationships. As Walker describes it, the two most fundamental categories of womanhood defined under male-dominated heterosexuality are bitches and wives. The first category is composed of white women; the second is made up of black women and is essentially the same as saying "mothers." The bitch in the book is Lynne, who in many ways is Meridian's antithetical parallel. A white woman, from the North, Jewish, a student and fellow Civil Rights worker, Lynne is the third factor in a triangular love relationship that includes Meridian and Truman, also a Civil Rights worker and the man both Lynne and Meridian love. The tension produced by love and jealousy is the ground on which Walker examines social categories and defines the process through which Meridian eventually liberates herself from male sexual domination.

Meridian begins her adult life a high-school dropout and teenage mother married to a restaurant busboy. Motherhood for Meridian is fraught with contradictory impulses. Caressing her child's body, she imagines that her fingers have scratched his flesh to the bone. At other times, she thinks of drowning her baby; when not fantasizing her child's murder, she dreams of suicide. Murder and suicide are the emotional articulation of social realities. This is the experience of futility—the mother's purposelessness as an individual, whose only function is to add yet another little body to the massive black underclass, and the child's bankrupt future, another faceless menial laborer.

In contrast to the futility is the one moment—equally profound for its singularity—when Meridian beholds her child with loving wonderment and sees him as a spontaneous, unasked-for gift, absolutely unique and whole. In response to the possibility for her child's selfhood and in recognition of her own desperate need to redefine her life's course, Meridian chooses to give her child away when, as if by miracle, her high IQ makes her a college candidate. In relinquishing her child, Meridian recognizes her relationship to the history of black motherhood, which, under slavery, defined the black woman's struggle to keep her children as a radical act, making the mother liable for a beating or worse; as well as to the time of freedom, which, in giving black women the right to keep their children, provided the fetters of enslavement to poverty and sexism. Meridian's mother is very much a part of this tradition. Although morally outraged at her daughter's decision to "abandon" her child, the mother exemplifies the plight of black mothers, "buried alive, walled away from her own life, brick by brick" (M, 51) with the birth of each successive child.

In giving her child away, Meridian makes it clear that mothering, as it has been defined by heterosexual relationships in racist society, is the single most insurmountable obstacle to a black woman's self-affirmation. Only by refusing ever to be a mother in the particular can she carve out a new social function, which includes a form of mothering, but in the larger sense of an individual's caring for her community. We get a sense of what this might involve when Meridian first appears in the novel leading a band of children in demonstration. But for the most part, Meridian's practice is less an indication of future possibilities and more a critique of the way heterosexual relationships have individualized a woman's relationship to *her* children, making them *her* property. This is the mother-child relationship that Meridian violently denies for herself when, becoming pregnant for a second time, she chooses to abort her lover's baby. Her decision is also a dramatic refutation of Truman's overtly male-chauvinist invitation to "have [his] beautiful black babies" (M, 116) for the revolution. For Meridian, the subsequent decision to have her tubes tied represents another step in the direction toward a new form of womanhood where heterosexuality will not be the means toward oppression but a mode within which sexual partners will one day set each other free. But for the time being, her espousal of a selfless, nunlike celibacy suggests that the day is a long way off.

For Lynne,[7] however, heterosexuality, complicated by the pressures on the biracial couple in a racist society, leads not to liberation and the affirmation of a new social mode, but rather the rock-bottom debasement of self. Notwithstanding her marriage to Truman, Lynne will always be the white bitch, and notwithstanding their child's African name, Camara, the mulatto does not represent a hope for a nonracist future. This is because American society—before, during, and after Civil Rights—remains racist and sexist. Camara's brutal murder graphically puts an end to any liberal thoughts about a new, hybridized society of the future. The death of this child—and all the book's children, either by abortion or murder—dramatizes Walker's radical intuition that the future as something positive and new cannot be produced out of genetic or personal terms, but demands, as Black Elk saw it, the selfless involvement of the individual with the community. When Truman criticizes Meridian for never having loved him, she responds, "I set you free" (M, 216). Meridian has chosen to relinquish personal and sexual relationships, which in this society cannot help but be the means and form of a woman's oppression, as a way of advancing her own struggle—and that of her loved ones—toward their liberation.

For the most part, Walker's writing is not figural, but there is in *Meridian* one very important metaphor, whose function is to synthesize the many levels of Meridian's struggle. This is the significance of Meridian's sickness, which goes by no medical name but is characterized by dizziness, temporary blindness, swooning faints, loss of hair, paralysis, and general bodily weakness. The illness strikes Meridian immediately after she first sees the Wild Child. Because many of the symptoms coincide with her childhood experiences of mystical ecstasy, the illness is a link between her early confrontation with cultural ideology and her later struggle as an adult against social and sexual oppression, typified by the plight of the Wild Child. The illness allows the reader to perceive at the level of experience the absolute energy-draining work of political praxis, as with each demonstration Meridian must struggle to regain her vanquished strength, patiently forcing her paralyzed limbs to work again. Meridian's trademark, a visored cap to cover her baldness, articulates the contradictory notions attached to a black woman's hair—her crowning glory and sign of sexuality—for which the head rag was both a proclamation and refutation. With each confrontation with white male authority—be it under the abortionist's knife or facing down an army tank—Meridian's swoon and faint proclaim not surrender but absolute commitment to the struggle. Coming back to consciousness, Meridian awakens to find the struggle—an ongoing process—renewed on a higher, more exacting level.

At the novel's conclusion, Walker gives us to understand that Meridian has mastered not the whole struggle but herself in that struggle. Rid of the sickness, her woolly head restored, she discards her cap and packs her bag to set out once again on the road to confrontation. Although one individual's coming to grips with self can be a lesson for others, it cannot be their solution. The novel closes on Truman, dizzily crawling into Meridian's sleeping bag, pulling her cap upon his head, and accepting for himself the long process of her struggle. The transition from Meridian to Truman lifts the book out of its sexual polarization and suggests that everyone regardless of socially ascribed sex roles, must work to deessentialize sex. Now it will be Truman who works for the community and in its care to bring the collective dream into being.

Although not by his choosing, Truman, at book's end, is no longer capable of being perceived either as a lover or a father. The course of Meridian's struggle to liberate herself from sexually prescribed categories has been the means for Truman's unwitting relinquishment of positions from which men have traditionally exerted domination. The transcendence of sexual domination undermines other forms of domination including racism, but this does not mean that race itself has been neutralized. Rather, blackness is affirmed. Meridian's new crop of woolly hair testifies directly to her renewal as a black woman. Nor has transcendence brought about Meridian's separation from the community, whose coherent presence has always been the novel's core. In contrast to the strength of the black presence, white people enter *Meridian* incidentally and are always perceived as individuals, bereft of any relationship with their own community. Almost freakish in their singularity and behavior, white people in general closely approximate their symbolic representation in the form of a mummified white woman, a sideshow attraction, whose husband carts her from town to town earning money off her exhibition.

Walker's affirmation of blackness uses racially specific traits not to define a form of black racism but to delineate the look of a class. Black is the color of the underclass. And all Walker's women are peasants, from Celie in *The Color Purple*, to Ruth's mother and grandmother in *The Third Life of Grange Copeland* and Meridian's female forebears. Bound to the land and their husbands (or fathers), worn by toil in the fields and the demands of childbearing, these women are the underclass of the underclass. This is why literacy and education are so crucial to the way Walker depicts the process of liberation. Her radical understanding of education lies at the heart of literacy campaigns from revolutionary Angola to Grenada and Nicaragua. Clearly, the ability to raise questions, to objectify contradictions, is only possible when Celie begins writing her letters. Similarly, for Meridian, education (notwithstanding its inspiration in liberalism) and the academic institution (notwithstanding its foundation in elitism) offer the means for confronting social and sexual contradictions that she, as a black teenage mother, would not have been able to articulate—either for herself or anyone else.[8]

Walker elaborated on the importance of class and the role of women in class politics in a workshop on black women writers held at Yale University (spring 1982). She stressed the significance of rediscovering Agnes Smedley, particularly Smedley's description of Chinese women during the years of the Revolution. Both Smedley and Walker would agree that the radical transformation of society can only be achieved when the bottom-most rung attains liberation; in fact, the wellspring of revolution is the rebellion of the peasant class. This is the great historical lesson of revolution in the twentieth century from China to Cuba and Central America. And it lies at the heart of all Smedley's "sketches" of women revolutionaries, who, when their class background and education more closely approximate Meridian's, must, like Walker's character, turn to the people and be one with their struggle. The individual who becomes separate from the peasantry is truly lost, like Walker's Lynne, who never outgrew her liberal background and the tendency to see black people as works of art; and Smedley's the "Living Dead," women reclaimed by the aristocracy and abandoned to opium dreams or so traumatized by the White Terror that they wander about dazed.

There is a great deal of similarity between the real-life Smedley and the fictional Meridian—and her autobiographical inspiration, Walker herself. Smedley, born in the South (Missouri), was also a peasant woman. Her childhood grounded in poverty, she, although white, knew a form of enslavement when, at the age of eleven, she was hired out as a domestic. Education and, later, leftist politics were her way up and out of poverty, just as writing was her way back to the people. Always an advocate of feminism, both in journalism and in fiction, Smedley, like Walker, depicts the contradictions of womanhood as they relate to abortion, birth control, and mothering. Finally, although Smedley's chosen community was revolutionary China, her relationship to that community as a foreigner and an intellectual bears striking similarity to Meridian's relationship to her community.

Perhaps the best way to characterize all three—Smedley, Meridian, and Walker—is with the title of one of Walker's collections of poems: *Revolutionary Petunias*. It captures the spirit of revolutionary women both in beauty and in struggle. Certainly, there was a great deal of flamboyance in Agnes Smedley as she donned a Red Army uniform and marched into Xi'an. Rather than a simplistic identification with the Communist forces, her act was intended to draw the attention of the world press (which it did) and to articulate a joyous celebration of struggle (which it still does) in the linguistics of gesture and playacting often used by women in lieu of those modes of communication, like speech and writing, that have been traditionally defined by male discourse. This is a form of revolutionary praxis very like the moment when Meridian, at the head of a pack of kids, faces down the town militia and a World War II tank. Not to be confused with flower children and the politics of counterculture, "Revolutionary Petunias" are those women, who, with grace, strength, and imagination, have put their lives on the line.

6. Problematizing the Individual

Toni Cade Bambara's Stories for the Revolution

Toni Cade Bambara's novel *The Salt Eaters*[1] represents the attempt to link the spirit of black activism generated during the sixties to the very different political and social situation defined by the eighties. The swing toward political conservatism in national politics makes this a project fraught with problems and frustration. I know of no other novel that so poignantly yearns for cataclysmic social upheaval and understands so clearly the roots of black people's oppression in post–Civil Rights American society. It seems, in reading the novel, that revolution is only pages away. But for all its yearning and insight, the novel fails to culminate in revolution, fails even to suggest how social change might be produced.

The reasons why this is so derive from the broadly felt political dismay of the post-Vietnam years and include the recognition among radical leaders that the political movements organized around minority oppression—gays, students, blacks, and women—which led the challenge against state capitalism during the late sixties, have failed to achieve the radical transformation of society. Bambara's novel ponders the shortcomings of minority political movements as it describes the futility felt by black community leaders in their attempts to renew the links with groups identified as "the Puerto Rican Nationalist Party," "La Raza Unida Groups," "the American Indian Movement," as well as the "loose, informal network of medicine people throughout the communities of color" (SE, 91).

The area in which the novel most senses and attempts to define the breakdown in black political activism is within the black community itself. Portraying it as having lost cohesion, Bambara focuses on the relationship between the community and its leaders. The Salt Eaters is in many ways a sad sequel to Meridian, not because Bambara is any less gifted a writer than Walker, but because the reciprocal relationship between the community and its revolutionary leader and the implicit understanding that their combined struggle will bring a transformed future into being no longer exist for the novel's Meridian-like figure, Velma Henry. At the opening of the novel, we find Velma, perched on a stool in an infirmary, deeply alienated, and only beginning to emerge from a state of near-catatonia—produced, not as the result of the violent political confrontations that would throw Meridian into exhausted swoons, but as the result of a failed suicide attempt. In questioning why Velma would want to kill herself, we as readers are led to scrutinize more than her personal relationships with husband, child, lover, and sisters in struggle. We are brought finally to grasp the personal as manifestation of the political.

The opening scene of The Salt Eaters swells with a cacophony of voices and stories. It is as if we were inside of Velma Henry's numbed consciousness, beginning to awaken from a gas-induced stupor, and only mildly aware of the many witnesses to her healing. Or perhaps our perception of the scene is more closely aligned with Minnie Ransom, the healer, whose hands and urgent pleas attempt to pull Velma back into life's flow. In any case, the jumble of voices encircling Velma and her healer, representing a varied collection of individuals whose present observations intersect with remembered bits from their separate pasts, produces a highly fragmented narrative context. The confusion is apt to overwhelm even the most skilled and persistent readers of modernist novels. Out of the cacophony emerges Smitty, beaten to a pulp during a street demonstration. There, too, is his mother, Sophie Haywood, in jail, face down on an iron cot, also being beaten. These are the voices and visions from the past. Interrupting them are narrative bits drawn from a more personal register as Velma remembers a heated conversation with her husband. From the present emerge the voices of the infirmary staff, taking bets on how long it will take Minnie Ransom to perform the cure: "Doc" Serge, a former gangster and pimp who now runs the infirmary; a group of visiting medical technicians and doctors, whose comments register their skepticism for the union of medicine and folk healing; and finally a soon-to-be teenage mother and her maybe-future husband, whose interior monologues combine personal preoccupations with mystical future visions. From the trivial to the profound, from history-making incidents to merely shooting the breeze, everything merges, converges, and impinges on the scene and the possibilities for Velma's recovery.

The metaphor of the individual's relationship to community could not be more explicit. If Velma Henry embodies the revolutionary leader, alone and in crisis, then the cacophony is the community, or, rather, it is the narrative jumble that would be reshaped in a meaningful way if the community were strong, supportive, and cohesive. The fragmentation and confusion of the community is so strongly felt in this text that the image of social cacophony, defined here in the infirmary, is later reproduced in other scenes from the novel, once on board a bus and again at a sidewalk café. This is the novel's traumatic metaphor with which it grapples in the hopes of finding resolution—some new image of social relations—only to return again to the old and problematical formula. In its depiction of a busload of passengers, the novel raises an important issue for politics in the eighties—that is, the impossibility of judging an individual's political allegiance on the basis of race or ethnicity. The social cacophony on board the bus includes its driver, Fred Hoyt, a black man, whose racist attitudes toward some of his "colored" pas-

sengers might just as easily have been formed inside a white consciousness; the Seven Sisters theater troupe, a multiethnic group
whose politics tend toward the ecological and mystical; a group
of white musicians, practitioners of black music; and, finally,
"two fat ladies," whose race, class, and culture seem to have
been absorbed by the amorphous category of housewife. The red-
neck musicians demonstrate that cultural interest need not coincide with political support. The bus driver's attitudes under-
cut the assumption of black solidarity with the Third World.
The bus is finally a randomly assembled, multiracial noncom-
munity evocative of the many social groupings possible in contemporary urban settings.

This is equally true of the scene at the sidewalk café. Here, the
Seven Sisters theater troupe reassembles for lunch, tables away
from a group of engineers from the local pollution-producing and
highly exploitative chemical plant, tables away from two black
women radicals. While the theater troupe plots its antinuke offering, the engineers play their version of global annihilation,
and the radical women discuss the nuts and bolts of community
organizing. For the most part, the tables define separate islands
of conversation and political allegiance, except during fleeting
moments when the Japanese "Sister of the Rice" shares suggestive glances with the Japanese chemical engineer (a gesture intended as an ironic device underscoring the error of assuming a
shared politics on a purely ethnic basis).

In all the novel's metaphors for society, the infirmary, the bus,
the sidewalk café, Bambara defines focal points in the larger social context that might one day be defined by community. Such
a community would not assume race as its primary factor, but
would draw on allegiances between racially defined groups and
the nascent politics of antinuclear and cultural movements.
These will provide the glue that will bring together the community of action. Such a community never comes together during
the space of the novel; rather, we feel its lack at each of the hectic sites where social cacophony prevails.

The images of infirmary, bus, and café illustrate another problem bearing on the formation of a black political community—namely, intervention from the outside. The community has itself become more cosmopolitan, particularly since the sixties, opening itself to Northern white Civil Rights workers and the struggles of Third World peoples. The image of a black community as it has been traditionally defined by small-town and urban ghetto may no longer symbolize the community of the eighties. During this era and as a result of the migration of corporate industry to the South, the black community has been subjected to another form of outside influence: colonization by the forces of industrial capitalism. The infirmary, the bus, and the café—each includes a representative of institutionalized authority, white supremacy, or corporate economics. The penetration of these forces produces a complex set of social relationships and makes it impossible to wage the simple, straightforward tactics of oppositional politics. In the society of the eighties, the brown-skinned woman with an antinuke T-shirt may not be willing to fight in the streets, whereas the white-skinned and deeply alienated corporate executive might be willing to blow up the company.

The Salt Eaters depicts a moment when class alliances are not discernible for the lack of political polarization. This sets the novel dramatically apart from Bambara's earlier writing, influenced by the clear-cut politics of the late sixties and early seventies. I suggest we compare the novel to some of Bambara's short stories as a way of defining the transformation in political climate. Stories like "The Organizer's Wife" from *The Sea Birds Are Still Alive*[2] portray a society gripped by the head-on confrontation between small landowners and tenant farmers pitted against an invading corporation, which is intent on turning the town into a quarry. One imagines giant rock-eating equipment gouging the ground out from under people's houses. The class lines of confrontation are clear; nevertheless, there are certain elements in the story that Bambara will develop as the basis for complication in her later writing, becoming fully realized in *The Salt Eaters*. For instance, the local black minister, who allies with the corporation and renounces his parishioners' interests, prefigures the black bourgeosie and underscores once more the error of assuming political commitment on the basis of race. Another factor that contributes to the story's hard-edged oppositional clarity, but will no longer obtain for Bambara's recent writing, is the focus on a moment in black politics when sexually defined roles in political practice were sharply drawn. Actually, the story depicts a moment after which it will no longer be possible to cast black women merely in supportive roles. Yet the implications of black women's political activism during and after the Civil Rights and Black Power movements have not yet been fully developed in terms of the story's critique of sexuality and the politics of sex. In focusing on one woman's politicization, the story ends at the moment when the organizer's wife relinquishes her loving dependency on her husband and comes to recognize herself in a politically active role that will unite her in love and responsibility with husband and community.

The Salt Eaters takes up the question of sex-defined roles where "The Organizer's Wife" leaves off. The story ends on the dawn of renewed political struggle, the woman now fully aware and uplifted by the recognition of her "input." The novel opens some fifteen years later with a group of radical women who have long been political activists and have come to realize that all their input has produced is a self-serving and egotistical black male leadership, given to silk pajamas, hotel suites, and limousines, while the women have suffered the ignominies of muddy marches and tent cities. Bambara's depiction of the typical black male politician is scathing in its cynicism:

> Some leader. He looked a bit like King, had a delivery similar to Malcolm's, dressed like Stokely, had glasses like Rap, but she'd never heard him say anything useful or offensive. But what a voice. And what a good press agent. And the

people had bought him. What a disaster. But what a voice. He rolled out his r's like the quality yardgoods he once had to yank from the bolts of cloth in his father's store in Brunswick, Georgia, till the day an anthropologist walked in with tape recorder and camera, doing some work on Jekyll Island Blacks and would he be so kind as to answer a few questions about the lore and legends of the island folks, and "discovered" him and launched him into prominence. "Leader. Sheeet." (*SE*, 35–36)

Although the community might be blamed for accepting a commodity as its leader, it is clear that forces larger than the community have facilitated his rise to power. Chosen for his media potential, the leader has been programmed and packaged to offer a perfect amalgam of political signifiers—all stripped of threatening content. Bambara's parable suggests that the commodity form may well represent the most advanced stage of capitalism's colonization of the black community.

Although the penetration of corporate capital capable of transforming a town into a strip mine and the commodification of social and political forms represent the most obvious forms of colonization, Bambara questions other processes, which tend to go unnoticed and are less readily opposed, particularly when these are the result of liberal government policies. Often the use of public monies to establish institutions and programs "for the good of the people" functions to perpetuate control and domination. But such programs may also be the means through which community leaders may evolve progressive social forms and activities. Bambara's story "Broken Field Running" describes a black urban setting, which at one time probably presented an image of social cohesion (small shops and walk-up flats, bars and restaurants), but now, with the help of corporate and government investment, has become an architectural and social hodgepodge, where zones of "renewal" interrupt the once-familiar neighborhood. The story follows two teachers, who, while escorting a group of young students to their homes, traverse the black neighborhood commenting on its deformation. Whereas the museum, housing an African art exhibit, represents government intervention in its positive form, the PAL discount store and windowless bank facade demonstrate the monstrosities of corporate colonization. So, too, the architecture of the projects provides ample space for "drug dealers," "take-off artists," "bullies," and "vipers" (SB, 45) while boxing in and fragmenting the residents, denying them—particularly their children—the space for fulfillment and play. As bad as the housing projects are, the school, an out-and-out prison, is worse:

> Cement grounds, hard, cold, treeless, shadowless, no hiding places or clustering places for plotting and scheming or just getting together. The building squats on an angle, as though snubbing the rest of the neighborhood, giving a cold shoulder, isolating itself, separating its inmates from the rest of the folks. (SB, 64–65)

Bisected, trisected, and quadrisected by corporate and federal money, the neighborhood is torn up and rebuilt on an inhuman plan whose purpose is control rather than development. The spatial image of the neighborhood, truly a "broken field," metaphorizes the sundering of social relationships wrought by the forces of late-twentieth-century colonization. Yet this bombed-out zone is also the social terrain out of which Bambara's revolutionary teachers hope to bring the utopian future into being. As one of the children puts it,

> "We won't mind the snow and the wind then,"... "Cause everybody'll have warm clothes and we'll all trust each other and can stop at anybody's house for hot chocolate cause won't nobody be scared or selfish. Won't even be locks on the doors. And every sister will be my mother." (SB, 69)

When the same child goes on to ask, "Will the new time come soon?", her teacher is able to respond, "It's here already...Because the new people, the new commitment, the new way is already here" (*SB*, 69). The teacher's vision, which creates a utopian vision in the midst of an expropriated neighborhood, is not an extreme example of social blindness. Rather, as he works with children, the embodiments of the future, causing them to see the inhumanity of "progress" (ghettoization, poverty, dehumanization), he makes the contradictions of capitalism forever fresh, forever raw in his students' minds. In asking simple questions such as why the project architects chose not to include restrooms on the ground floor, the teacher asks the students to ponder the lives of the elderly and women with children. Laying bare the contradictions of daily life prevents their becoming naturalized. Failure to raise the questions would condemn the children of tomorrow to accept the horrors of broken field living as normal. The teacher's commitment to the future and his refusal of complacency enable the story's claim for utopia.

This is not the case in *The Salt Eaters*, where the urban environment is perceived through the consciousness of a black bus driver, who, as he drives, becomes increasingly nauseous and disoriented. His route takes him across a scene of total urban transformation where gentrification means razing the neighborhood. Because these changes are filtered through the private nightmare of the bus driver they do not have the power to define contradiction.

> Stores gutted, car shells overturned, a playground of rust and twisted steel. Mounds of broken green bottle glass, rusted bedsprings, bald tires, doors off their hinges leaning in the wind, flower-pot shards and new looking brick and lumber strewn about but not haphazardly, as if a crew had brushed them off with profit in mind. Panes of glass up against a half-wall for pickup later, looked like. A project not long ago put up was now this pile of rubble. And in the middle of it all a crater. He specially did not want to look at that. Not in all this heat. Not with his stomach churning up the lousy lunch. (*SE*, 71–72)

Outside of the passing reference to a "crew," no agent of destruction is defined. This gives the impression that the leveling of the neighborhood has been the result of a natural cataclysm rather than urban renewal. The transformation from housing project to crater, explained by a litany of well-worn slogans, "Redevelopment. Progress. The master plan" (SE, 72), fails to express the devastating impact such a transformation has on the people involved. In fact, people have been doubly removed from the scene. No longer present in the objects of daily life—the beer and wine they might have consumed, the cars they might have driven, or the beds they might have slept and made love in—the people have become a sundered memory whose lives are as irretrievable as a whole bottle from the shards.

Even though the bus driver is a sympathetic and critical onlooker, his attitude is distanced. He, unlike the teachers in Bambara's earlier story, is not committed to bring the future into being through painstaking teaching and community work. Instead, ground down by years of work for a company that now threatens to fire him, the bus driver can muster but one gesture of defiance—to suck his teeth. Instead of envisioning the revolution in the present, the bus driver escapes into fantasies, envisioning himself a gun-toting revolutionary:

> Him riding shotgun on a derrick and crane. New housing going up and him going up in a glass elevator with a hard hat on. Schools, playgrounds, stores, clinics. And they, the older men the young ones were quick to call over the hill and through, would defend it all with guns. (SE, 72)

This is a narrative whose dreams do not flow from contradiction transcended. It sees and records without really understanding. Bouncing from images of destruction to the plastic images of shopping mall and suburbs, "Blonds with dogs on leashes and teenage kids on bikes" (SE, 72), the change is felt to be inevitable.

The readers of The Salt Eaters, like the passengers on Fred

Hoyt's bus, travel through a narrative whose disarray suggests another point of difference between the novel and Bambara's earlier writing. Whereas the short stories are multiple fragments and figures that may be assembled into interpretive wholes and, thus, exemplify literary modernism, the novel approximates a postmodern narrative, whose profuse array of disconnected detail denies interpretation and suggests a world where meaning no longer pertains. In *The Salt Eaters*, Fred Hoyt and Campbell, the waiter at the sidewalk café, occupy key positions in relation to the possibility for constructing a narrative. They are potential narrative makers whose thought and actions might, in another textual form, create the links between the otherwise isolated fragments of incidents and description. However, as Campbell weaves his way in and out and around the tables at the restaurant, overhearing bits of conversation, neither his movements nor his conscious train of thought produce narrative continuity. Instead, he, like the bus driver, remains one more isolated individual—himself a narrative bit—whose mobility only serves to heighten our awareness of the scene's overall discontinuity. The notion of a mobile character, whose function is to assemble narrative and experiential fragments, lacking in Bambara's novel, is, however, not foreign to the history of black women's writing. In *Mules and Men*, Hurston's anthology of black folktales, the author's narrative persona provides the contextual links between her informants' stories, thus creating the sort of narrative glue Bambara's mobile characters fail to achieve. Traveling the back roads from town to town and story to story, Hurston weaves her voice in and out and around her collected tales, textualizing black rural Southern tradition. Hurston's achievement of narrative continuity out of discontinuous stories and experience is all the more striking given the fact that her text bridges much larger discontinuities, including the separations between South and North, and all the economic and racial inequalities associated with these zones. The fact that neither of Bambara's potential narrators can link the fragments drawn from the stories and experience of their social context suggests how deeply sundered contemporary society has become. Here, disparate social moments—the industrial, cultural, ethnic, economic—seem to deny the possibility of a totalizing perception of society.

The transformation in the composition and terrain of the community creates deep frustrations for the individual who would be leader. During periods of transition, the terms of previous political struggles become disengaged from the historical context that shaped them. Meanwhile the terms crucial to the next political contest have not yet emerged. During such periods, the individual revolutionary leader is cast in sharp relief against a community locked in turmoil but going nowhere. The individual comes under scrutiny in ways not possible at times of strong community cohesion and activism. Periods of quandary, slackening, or redefinition problematize the radical individual, calling into question the terms of his or her relationship to the group. One of the problems made manifest is the degree to which the role of the revolutionary leader and our perception of the leader are, in Western society, influenced by the ideology of individualism. Alice Walker's Meridian, as she is conceptualized within the political framework of the sixties, is really no less mired in the problems related to Western individualism than is Bambara's Velma Henry. What makes our perception of the two protagonists so different is that Meridian's activism and her reciprocal relationship to the Southern black community prevent her role as an individual from becoming overly central. Even though Velma Henry confronts many of the same problems Merdian had to deal with, including sexism in the community and racism in society, Meridian's struggle was part of an ongoing movement into a future that was as much her community's as her own, a future that of necessity would abolish the dichotomy between leader and led. In contrast, Velma Henry is cast as an isolated revolutionary, loosely connected with other more or less alienated radicals—all of whom are currently uncertain of their relationship to grass-roots organizing and the larger political battles to be waged. In problematizing the individual, *The Salt Eaters* demands that we question the basis for renewed political activity in the eighties, and at the same time, it asks us to reevaluate the politics of the sixties and seventies. In so doing, we are led to examine the notion of leadership and the role of the individual revolutionary even though these were not seen as the most pressing problems during the sixties. In a purely literary context, the many lone and frustrated radicals we find in *The Salt Eaters* demand that we as readers return to Bambara's earlier writing, focusing on the definition of the individual in these texts where individualism was not yet felt to be a problem.

Bambara's earliest collection of stories, *Gorilla, My Love*,[3] presents situations where individual characters are sharply defined, but the notion of the individual is not problematized. Stories where the evocation of the individual is the strongest, such as "Raymond's Run" and "Gorilla, My Love," are narrated in the first person from the point of view of Hazel, Bambara's spunky child persona. These stories define a resourceful, witty, and courageous young girl, similar to the strong young girls we find in Morrison's first novels: Claudia, from *The Bluest Eye*, and Sula. In their portrayals of preadolescent girls, drawn from their own childhoods, black women writers like Bambara, Morrison, and Marshall have fashioned a highly perceptive means for exposing the contradictions of capitalist society, which is cast as the discontinuity between the child's perception of the choices made by adults in a given situation and the child's own critical apprehension of the situation. The child's radical perception of the influence of racial, sexual, and economic inequalities on the world of adults is possible because, although the child is influenced by the same social forces, she is not yet wholly inscribed within their contradictions because she is not yet a producer or reproducer of the system. Contradiction, revealed through the eyes of the child narrator, has the power of freshness, which compels the reader to critical attention. In contrast, when contradiction is recorded by an adult character, it is apt to seem so straightforward, so commonplace, so inextricably oppressive as to deny contestation and change.

In the work of Morrison and Bambara, the portrayal of young girls bristles with irrepressible energy. Morrison's Sula and Claudia and Bambara's Hazel are deeply inquisitive and often sharply critical of established order, fearless in the face of authority, and profoundly sensitive to other people's needs and desires. The only thing that differentiates Bambara's Hazel from Morrison's young girls is the important sisterly relationship between Morrison's characters. In *The Bluest Eye*, Claudia is seconded and supported by her real sister, Frieda; Sula's comrade in struggle is her age- and soulmate, Nel. In contrast, Bambara's Hazel, although shown in gratifying and strong relationships with friends and family members, is defined as a separate and strong individual, possessed of a clearly defined consciousness. The difference is important to our development of the political implications associated with the individual. Although Morrison's sisterly characters are no less strong for the companionship than is Bambara's Hazel in her aggressive solitude, Morrison's young girls confront life on a dialogical and dialectical basis. Nel and Sula, Frieda and Claudia function as thesis and antithesis in the dialectical understanding of contradiction. Their relationship articulates a dynamic approach toward the problems of authority, racism, and sexual oppression. In conversation, discussing and interpreting the words and actions of adults, Morrison's sisters suggest the nucleus of a larger, although not yet realized, community. On the other hand, Bambara's individual protagonist, set dramatically against society's authority figures, and only loosely associated with peers and family, is the prototype for the isolated revolutionary in *The Salt Eaters*.

"Raymond's Run" focuses on Hazel, the eight-year-old, fifty-yard dash specialist. As she puts it, "I am Miss Quicksilver herself" (*GML*, 27); "I always win cause I'm the best" (*GML*, 26). Such sentiments expressive of the child's self-pride might, in an adult political leader, produce blind spots and hinder alliances.

Taking her time getting ready for the big May Day race, Hazel is Miss Self-Confidence herself. Lounging about in the grass rather than nervously exercising before her event, Hazel projects a cool exterior, whose strength of purpose the narrative affirms in its simple, declamatory style. Identity is extremely important to Hazel. To parents who would have her dress up like a strawberry for the festival, she announces, "I do not dance on my toes. I run. That is what I am all about" (GML, 26). The short sentences, the repetition of the affirming, "I am" throughout, and the attention Hazel gives to her full name, "Miss Hazel Elizabeth Deborah Parker. (Dig that)" (GML, 32) underscore the centrality of self, which, in this story, is appropriate for the child's point of view and in response to the competitive nature of the race and the larger social forces that the May Day celebration embodies.

Although Hazel is pitted against other runners, the real focus of her competitive spirit is the race official, who taunts and inferiorizes her by using her nickname, "Squeaky," when preparing to announce her event. He also has the audacity to suggest she let some other runner win. Although the suggestion is couched in terms of fairness, it actually articulates the manipulative control figures of authority seek to exercise in any given situation. Although it is quite clear that the official represents "grown-up" authority, established law and order, and the power to dominate, and that he is a man, Bambara does not underscore the fact that he is black. Aside from the general notion of black pride evoked by Hazel as an accomplished runner, race and racial prejudice are not specifically at issue in the story. Rather, Hazel contests political authority as it is invested in male figures and she does so on the basis of her performance and her insistence on the use of her proper name. These are the story's contestatory elements, which shape the individual's oppositional stance. For its sense of politics as opposition and contestation, the story is very much a product of the sixties.

However, "Raymond's Run" includes other incipient possibilities. These are less developed than its oppositional motif, but they have important implications for bringing the individual out of potential isolation and into association with a larger community. In its portrayal of Hazel's rivalry with the second-place runner, Gretchen P. Lewis, the story examines the transformation from antagonism to mutual appreciation. Although Hazel and Gretchen never achieve a sisterly relationship, they do come to recognize each other with respect:

> We stand there with this big smile of respect between us. It's about as real a smile as girls can do for each other, considering we don't practice real smiling every day, you know, cause maybe we too busy being flowers or fairies or strawberries instead of something honest and worthy of respect . . . you know . . . like being people. (*GML*, 32)

Bambara's use of the word "worthy" calls to attention the devaluation of women in this society, who, from infants to adults, assume the dehumanized identities compatible with male domination. The smile defines a mode of exchange not inscribed within this society's economics of exchange. It establishes a bridge between equals and suggests the basis for a system of bonding between women, which will not include domination within it, but will oppose domination in society.

The other aspect that propels "Raymond's Run" out of an essentially individualist bias is Hazel's eventual recognition of her brother as a person rather than a objectified responsibility. The transition from Hazel's centrality to Raymond's potential, which gives the story its title, is, however, not fully realized until the conclusion. In winning the May Day race, Hazel comes to see that running need not be the sole source of her strength and identity. She might assume other roles, such as coaching her brother. Hazel's decision prefigures the crucial role that all teachers will play in Bambara's later writing about community leaders and organizers. In imagining herself allied with Gretchen, the two of them bringing out Raymond's potential, Hazel prefigures the explicitly revolutionary characters found in Bambara's more recent collection of stories: *The Sea Birds Are Still Alive*.

However, the most important aspect of Hazel's regard for Raymond has to do with her ability to envision a future for her brother. Raymond is mentally retarded and, according to our society's criteria, ought to be barred from achieving an active and satisfying role. Rather than casting Hazel's care for her brother in terms of altruism, which would affirm certain character traits ascribed to extraordinary individuals in bourgeois society, I think we should define Hazel's vision of her brother as a metaphor for black community. By comparison to white-dominated society, which practices the exclusion of its marginals, putting them in homes and institutions and jails, the alternative society defined by the black community would embrace all its members, allowing each to fulfill a self-sustaining and group-supporting role. In dominant white society, the tyranny of physical and mental perfection might be taken as a displaced expression of its racism.

When Hazel exclaims, "my brother Raymond, a great runner in the family tradition" (*GML*, 32), she underscores another aspect central to Bambara's early definition of the individual's relationship to the larger group. In her first stories, the family—particularly the extended family—functions as a collectivity of support and reservoir of history and tradition in much the same way as the community of neighborhood or town will function in the more recent fiction. The family is for the critically discerning child what the community will be for organizer and teacher.

Very often the child's task will be to raise the consciousness of family members, as in "Gorilla, My Love," one of Bambara's most engaging short stories. Its poignancy derives from the way the individual's relationship to the family is defined against the influence of larger social forces that penetrate and corrupt the family community. Told again from the child Hazel's point of view, the story exposes the lived experience of domination in a curious blend of insight and naiveté. Finally, for her unbending courage and for the demands she places on her community and expects its members to fulfill, Hazel is the child prototype of the adult radical Velma Henry. One might read "Gorilla, My Love" and *The Salt Eaters* as key markers on a historical time line spanning from the sixties to the eighties. Although the story's central problematic is straightforward and, like the sixties, conditioned by the politics of contestation and opposition, its sense of the influence of dominant ideology on the minority community defines Bambara's first attempt to come to grips with the more complicated issues that problematize her novel of the eighties.

"Gorilla, My Love" is composed of two narratives: a framing story focused on Hazel's betrayal by a family member, and an internal anecdote that tells of how Hazel was tricked by a theater manager. The story's parallel construction is the means for developing the connection between the relationships pertaining to capitalist society in general and those relationships within the black community that tend to reproduce forms of domination. The story opens with Hazel, her granddaddy, uncle, and little brother making a pecan-hauling run. Hazel's sense of self-importance is disrupted when her uncle announces from the backseat that he will soon be getting married. Apparently unmindful of the promise he gave his little niece to marry her when she grew up, the uncle has broken his bond and betrayed his commitment to Hazel. The story demands that we read both inside and outside the world of childhood, accepting the seriousness of the uncle's offence along with the condescension with which adults often treat children. The strength of the story resides in its translation of racist oppression in society at large into the child's experience of victimization by the laws and lies of adult society.

The story's social implications are revealed when Hazel, at the moment of her betrayal, recalls a similar incident that took place at a movie theater on Easter Sunday. Hazel, Big Brood, and Baby Jason had expected to see a movie about a gorilla, but ended up seeing the agony of Christ on the cross. Although the rational

or adult explanation might have it that Hazel misread the theater marquee, Hazel's interpretation places the blame on the
theater management, "if you say Gorilla, My Love, you suppose
to mean it" (GML, 17). Her response is the direct confrontation
with authority. Marching in on the theater manager, she demands
her money back, and when the manager refuses, she steals the
matches from his desk and lights a fire under the candy counter
that shuts the theater down for a week. Shaped by the politics of
the sixties, her action is contestatory, but it is also inscribed
within the modes of exchange defined by a money economy and
private property. Images evocative of the sixties appear elsewhere
in the story, such as the incipient image of community defined
by the kids' section at the theater, roped off and separated from
the society of adults. Convinced they have been tricked, the kids

> go wild. Yellin, booin, stompin and carryin on. Really to
> wake the man in the booth up there who musta went to
> sleep and put on the wrong reels. But no, cause he holler
> down to shut up and then he turn the sound up so we really
> gotta holler like crazy to even hear ourselves good. And the
> matron ropes off the children section and flashes her light
> all over the place and we yell some more and some kids slip
> under the rope and run up and down the aisle just to show
> it take more than some dusty ole velvet rope to tie us
> down. And I'm flingin the kid in front of me's popcorn.
> And Baby Jason kickin seats. And it's really somethin.
> (GML, 15)

Unarmed and throwing whatever comes to hand, surveyed with
searchlights, and bombarded by an audio barrage, the children
easily call to mind a group of sixties-style demonstrators, beseiged by police and their heavy-handed crowd-control tactics.
So, too, does Hazel's euphoric, "And it's really somethin," express the youthful spirit of sixties activists.

The story's most far-reaching implications turn, however, on
the relationship of naming to meaning—in other words, the
question of signifying. Hazel's contention is that the gap be-

tween the signifier and the signified must be annulled. Otherwise, to give an empty signifier in the place of a meaningful term constitutes lying, which in turn allows power and oppression to enter human relationships. Many times in the story, Hazel mentions the different names that family members have given her. Her granddaddy calls her "scout" as she reads the map on their pecan-hauling runs. Her mama calls her "Bad-bird" when she's caught in a bind and won't back down. And her Aunt Daisy calls her "Miss Muffin" (*GML*, 18). These names are situation-specific, and, while they indicate aspects of Hazel's identity, they do not represent Hazel as a self, capable of establishing promises or entering into contract with the community. On this point Hazel is adamant. "My name is Hazel. And what I mean is you said you were going to marry me when I grew up" (*GML*, 19). Leaving aside the specific question of marriage, what Hazel is demanding of her uncle is that their relationship *not* be inscribed within the commodified (she says "trickified") forms of exchanged defined under late capitalism and typified by the movie marquee whose separation between naming and meaning creates a space for the exercise of domination. Hazel's granddaddy attempts to resolve the contradiction by saying that Hunca Bubba (Hazel's childhood name for her uncle) made the promise, but Hunca Bubba has now become the more mature Jefferson Windsong Vale. The solution represents the splitting of individuals into many separate sets of relationships that, if the separate parts are taken as a whole, may be in conflict. Such a solution is possible only in a society where the commodity form, which in language produces empty signifiers, constitutes the relationship between people as well as their objects. For its linguistic insight, the story goes beyond its base in sixties-style politics and suggests the social relationships associated with the post-Vietnam years and the culture of advanced consumer capitalism. At the story's end, solidarity only exists between Hazel and her brother, Baby Jason. "I can't see for cryin. And Baby Jason cryin too. Cause he is my blood brother and understands that we must stick together or be forever lost" (*GML*, 20). With the larger community (in this case, the extended family) influenced and assimilated into the forces defining dominant society, only the smallest, most narrowly defined groups can prevail. The fragmented and besieged nucleus of a once-thriving community that concludes "Gorilla, My Love" is Bambara's starting point for *The Salt Eaters.*

In the dozen or so years between the publication of "Gorilla, My Love" and *The Salt Eaters,* Bambara published her most explicitly political stories in the collection *The Sea Birds Are Still Alive.* These stories develop the integral relationship between the revolutionary leader and the community. Significantly, the family, which functioned in *Gorilla, My Love* as the displaced representation of the black community, is abandoned—often thrown into question—while the notion of a collectivity expands into the community at large: the revolutionary band, the neighborhood, or small town. Two stories in particular problematize the family, criticizing male domination of the nuclear family and demonstrating the importance of developing child-rearing institutions in the community. One such story is "A Tender Man," which explores black male child abandonment. The protagonist, a guilt-ridden professional man, may seem atypical of the commonly held image of black men who have walked away from their fatherly responsibilities. In situating the problem of fathering within the black middle class rather than focusing on the poverty-striken and unemployed or perpetuating the image of black men as gamblers, boozers, and womanizers, Bambara demonstrates how all black family relationships have been affected by their inclusion within a dominating white capitalist society. In the story, racism is one of the factors that has driven a wedge between father and daughter. Feeling guilt over his relationship with a white woman, the child's mother, the father is incapable of imagining a future for his daughter or what his role as a future maker might be. Ambiguity, uncertainty, guilt—these are the lived experiences of people whom this society includes in its multiethnic rainbow, although excluding them from jobs, housing, and a future on the basis of race.

Another factor that in the story has severed father from daughter is capitalist society's exploitative use of a black male labor pool—in this case, a military labor pool. The man learns of his impending fatherhood while en route to the Bay of Pigs invasion. At the precise moment when he might assume a fatherly role, he sees himself transformed into a nonperson, a pawn in a global chess game. The secrecy of the mission erases the details of the event from official history and defines the man, whether he lives or dies, as a lie. Capitalism's use of young men, and particularly black men, to wage clandestine wars and wars shrouded in lies like Vietnam has created a perpetual class of fathers whose identity and basic humanity have been stripped from them.

In attempting to solve the problem of fathering, Bambara responds with an image of the future that greatly transcends the social relationships associated with bourgeois capitalism. Rather than calling for the restoration of fathering and the restructuring of the nuclear family, she redefines parenting, not as the function of individuals, be they mothers or fathers, but as the responsibility of a larger community group. She does so by demonstrating that all adults have a responsibility to develop a strong and positive sense of race and culture in the children who will make the world's future. She demands that we ask what the future of the story's child would be if she were forced to live out her mother's racial ignorance and prejudice. Her father as an individual cannot be her salvation; but he, as her father, can be made to see the error of his abandonment and the possibility of developing a nonpaternalistic form of fathering that would extend the role of parenting to brothers and sisters of the race, to schools and community workers.

The family comes under attack again in "A Girl's Story" from the same collection. In focusing on a young girl's first menstruation, the story demonstrates how male-dominated ideas about women's sexuality penetrate and inform the way women relate to their daughters, even in situations where no man is in the home. "A Girl's Story" is a parable depicting the brutality of mothering in a male-dominated society. Rae Ann's first menstruation is a lesson in victimization— first, by her grandmother, whose reaction to the bloody flow is to accuse Rae Ann of having had a coat-hanger abortion, and second, by her brother, who seconds the grandmother's assumptions, giving lurid details of her sexual relationships with boys. Acting as stand-ins for the absent father figure, Rae Ann's brother and grandmother—even though one is a boy and the other a woman—act to perpetuate male domination in the family. They perpetuate the inferiorization of women and their appropriation to domination as mindless and wanton sexual objects.

The image of the male-dominated nuclear family is, however, counterbalanced in the story by the positive portrayal of a very different mother figure. This is Dada Bibi, a teacher at the local community center, whose supportive relationship to Rae Ann is based on a deep—but nonpossessive—love. "You're becoming a woman and that's no private thing. It concerns us all who love you. Let's talk sometimes?" (SB, 155–56). Observations like these run throughout the narrative, exemplifying Dada Bibi's alternative form of mothering, even while Rae Ann hides from her grandmother and brother, knowing she must eventually face their rebukes. The teacher's words demystify male domination, showing that its power resides in the privatization of women, which makes women equivalent to property. Dada Bibi's vision points to a feminist society in which sharing between women of different generations will be based on the deprivatization of women's experience.

Bambara expands the function of mothering out of the family and into the community until, with "The Apprentice," she replaces the biological mother-child relationship with the learning and caring relationship between a middle-aged community organizer and her young apprentice. As she portrays them, the two characters come to embody the deepest dilemma Bambara faces as a writer—namely, how to bridge the gap between sixties activism and post-Vietnam uncertainty. Naomi, the organizer, sees the future in the present; her every discussion, project, or relationship is an enactment of revolution. In contrast, the young apprentice is a doubter. "What have I seen but junkies noddin in the alley, dudes steppin in my window to rip me off, folks that'd kill God for a quarter" (SB, 33). It isn't that Naomi overlooks grim social reality, but from her point of view the revolution is at hand. Political work, particularly at a time of great social misery and oppression, is revolutionary. In contrast, the apprentice conceptualizes the revolution as a single, verifiable moment: the moment of transformation, which obviously hasn't yet occurred and so must be somewhere in the future. The difference between the two versions of revolution is precisely the difference between the politics of the sixties, which saw every demonstration, every countercultural gesture, as part of an ongoing revolution, and the eighties, which as a time of transition and dismay, can at best posit the revolution somewhere around the corner.

"The Apprentice" provides an important point of comparison with *The Salt Eaters* both for its definition of a mutual relationship between the organizer and the community, which in the novel will no longer obtain, and for the depiction of the community itself as a cohesive unit. Whereas *The Salt Eaters* shows the space of the community as a loosely defined topography, which includes a number of varied autonomous zones—the bus, the infirmary, the café—"The Apprentice" describes a heterogeneous collectivity, whose focal points are equally representative of the whole and important for the reproduction of social life. As Naomi and her young disciple travel from old-folks home to the black lodge to the drive-in restaurant, their movement defines the extent of the community and binds its members together even as their conversations with retired people, brother Decker, and short-order cooks give shape to the community's future aspirations. This is not the case in *The Salt Eaters* where each of the loci defined by discussion is separate from the others, and where the organizer, the community's hope for cohesion, sits, immobilized, recovering from her attempted suicide. The difference resides again in the separation between the politics of the sixties, in which all social activity was defined as important precisely because it was embedded in daily life and therefore responsible for its reproduction and potentially capable of its transformation, and the politics of the eighties, where splintering leads to the overdetermination of certain social instances, making it seem that there must be some single event or situation magically capable of transforming the whole.

All the stories in *The Sea Birds Are Still Alive* participate in the definition of the individual's relation to the community without at the same time problematizing the notion of the individual. It is on this point that *The Salt Eaters* represents a sharp break in the development of Bambara's writing. Velma Henry's attempted suicide is a figural device for asking, in an agonizing way, what will be the terms of the individual's relationship to loved ones and community, to past tradition and future society. Suicide represents the individual's renunciation of any connection with society; it is the individual's ultimate statement of autonomy. The failure to commit suicide offers the group the opportunity to redefine itself, affirm its importance for the alienated individual, and bring her back into the collectivity. *The Salt Eaters*, which opens on Velma's healing and concludes with her cure, describes the process of the individual's rebirth into society. The yin and yang articulated by Velma's failed suicide balances the individual's possibility for achieving absolute autonomy against its antithesis, the dissolution of self within the group. The first gives rise to fascist fantasies; the second suggests Western liberalism's conception of communism. As metaphorized in its title, *The Salt Eaters* attempts to find a social alternative where the individual would be defined by neither extreme. One must eat salt to live. One must eat salt to be healed. As one of the novel's characters explains, "Remember Napoleon's army? Those frogs were dropping dead from scratches because their bodies were deprived of salt" (*SE*, 164). But too much salt is a poison. Crying out the body's salt is necessary. Just as the release of passion is necessary for the individual, so too is the diffusion of the one into the many necessary for the group's health. Retention, holding back, shoring up the self eventually produce the death of the individual and the sundering of the social fabric.

If we translate the rubric of *The Salt Eaters* back into Bambara's early short stories, we are apt to view the strength of the individual child characters more critically. The self-affirmation, pride, and courage that propel Hazel as a young girl become, in Velma Henry, the cause for frustration and anger. The strength of the individual in one situation precipitates the individual's breakdown in another. What has changed is not the individual so much as the society's ability to offer the individual a place where strength and action may find resonance. The fact that Velma can't shake the image of a certain black politician wearing Chinese pajamas, that she is haunted by it, and, like a traumatized person, repeatedly summons up this image of her betrayal should not be interpreted as an indication of Velma's emotional imbalance. Rather, it indicates to what extent her incisive anger has nowhere to go, can't strike a chord in the community, can't be resolved and put to rest by collective action.

As in her short stories, the social definition of mothering is the area where Bambara most scrutinizes the individual's relation to the group. However, in contrast to the short stories, where the mother-child relationship is described in purely social terms, the novel has a strong mythic dimension, which influences the portrayal of mothering and dovetails with the mystical aspect of its evocation of yin and yang. The mythic aspect also contributes to the novel's ambiguous conclusion when rain, wind, and trembling earth call on nature at all levels to act as substitute for the tremendous transformation we long to witness in society.

The most mythical of the novel's mother images, the one to

which Velma returns at the lowest moments during the process of her healing, is that of the "mud mothers" (*SE*, 255). It is interesting that Bambara never fully describes the "mud mothers." Rather, she allows us to flesh out the image, drawing on our store of nightmare ideology and popular-culture models. We are apt to imagine a barely discernible group of maternal primitives, writhing about, like tribal initiates in a muddy bath. Such an image combines the ideological representation of primitive society with Hollywoodesque portrayals of bodies sinking into quicksand. It articulates the child's repressed fear of the mother, whose overprotection might lead to smothering. And it articulates the individual's fear of being sucked down and incorporated into the vague mass of society.

The "mud mothers" are often depicted "painting the walls of a cave" (*SE*, 255), an activity of profound symbolic importance in relation to Bambara's project as a writer. Painting as a form of articulation summons up the long history of women's search for a mode of discourse not curtailed by men or inscribed within male-dominated society. Often denied access to speech and writing, women, particularly black women, have had to develop modes of expression in other artistic and folk forms. However, these have often gone unnoticed, relegated to the underside of history like these paintings on the walls of caves.[4] Significantly, Minnie Ransom's cure is intended not only to restore Velma to the community, but to give her a voice as well. During the process of her healing, Velma is encouraged to dance and to respond verbally to her healer. The moment of her cure finds Velma, her "head thrown back about to shout, to laugh, to sing" (*SE*, 295).

The most central of the novel's mother figures is, of course, Minnie Ransom, a bedangled and braceleted "spinster," who might best be characterized as a contemporary culture figure with connections to the mythic dimension. Folkloric as well as socially hip, she accompanies her cure with stereophonic jazz and refers to the music as a creation of the "loas" (*SE*, 54). Minnie is aided in her curing by another maternal figure, one whose relationship to myth and the folk tradition are much deeper. This is "Old Wife," Minnie's spirit guide, who, although she denies working in sorcery, comes to resemble an Afro-American root worker. In doubling the figure of the maternal healer, Bambara creates a link between present and past cultural practice and she suggests the incipient basis for sisterhood. The unity of purpose and the supportive interaction, as well as the lively banter and respectful rivalry, are all characteristics that would define a larger collectivity of women. Finally, in doubling the figure of the healer, Bambara creates a dialogue, demonstrating that healing is a process of working through. The healers in relation to the patient establish a dialectic in discourse and action.

There is yet another figure in the novel: Sophie Haywood, whose role as a midwife establishes a nominal connection with folk medicine and tradition, and whose work as an organizer and political activist push the function of mothering into a wholly new social space. With the creation of Sophie Haywood, Bambara seems to suggest the separation between the mainstream of folk tradition and political work. Not only are these areas divided for the most part, between Minnie and Sophie, but at the moment Minnie begins her cure, Sophie leaves the room, withdraws to "Doc" Serge's office where she holds a separate meditative vigil. The novel ends with the suggestion that Velma's future will involve a closer affiliation with Sophie. "Once Minnie brought Velma through perhaps the girl at last would be ready for training" (SE, 293). Sophie's thoughts summon up images from Bambara's earlier writing where the close association between student and teacher or organizer and apprentice gave shape to the future in faith and confidence.

That such a vision is not fully realized in The Salt Eaters has again to do with the great difference between the political climate of the sixties and that of the eighties. But rather than continuing to focus on the rupture between these two political moments as I have been developing the problem, I'd like to suggest another way of understanding the inconclusive nature of

The Salt Eaters. I suggest we position the novel in relation to a project that is not at all new, but found tremendous impetus in the sixties and continues, even in this era of political conservatism, to focus the energies of women radicals. I am referring to the feminist project to rewrite history from the point of view of women. Once we suspend a male-dominated view of history and its emphasis on the graphable, the chronological, the litany of events and leaders, then we create a space for women's history, whose movers and shapers have often gone unrecorded, leaving only the continuity of daily struggle. The difference between male- and female-defined histories is what Bambara is getting at when she contrasts the black political leader in silk pajamas, whose acts and pronouncements will make the news, with Velma and the other demonstrators, whose march and muddy encampment may go as unheeded as the women's pleas for medical attention, food, and clothing. The "mud mothers" is a compelling image because it is rooted in the suppression of women's history. It is the mud of erasure out of which women must struggle. But because we still live in a male-dominated society, it is not yet clear what history will be like when the continuity of suppressed voices becomes the means for knowing and explaining the course of history. This is the context out of which Bambara is writing. Seen from this perspective, her writing defines much more of a continuity from the short stories to the novel than is apparent when we judge her books purely on the basis of the rupture between sixties- and eighties-style politics.

Because society has for so long been explained from a male point of view, the movers and shapers of women's history are only partially visible. The desire to formulate a feminist perspective on history accounts for the centrality of mother figures in Bambara's writing. Her radicalism is to suggest how mothering, which in the nuclear family is necessary and acceptable to male-dominated society, might be extended into the community and transformed. Where we most feel the influence of male domination on the ability to envision alternative social forms defined by women is in Bambara's scant development of sisterly relations. We sense that sisterhood would include the intuitive closeness that links Velma to her sister, Palma; in the Seven Sisters theater group, we understand that sisterhood is lively, spontaneous, creative, and caring. Through these images, we glimpse possibilities and hope that the eighties will be the ground of their realization. The coming to fruition of women's history would redefine the past twenty years on the basis of continuity, rather than rupture.[5]

7. Envisioning the Future

The single most compelling aspect of black women's writing today is its ability to envision transformed human social relationships and the alternative futures these might shape. Only utopian science fiction like Marge Piercy's *Woman on the Edge of Time*,[1] equals black women's writing for its claim on future visions and these are often so highly evolved, so imaginatively transformed that they can no longer make manifest how utopia might be produced out of our own world's dehumanizing inequalities. In contrast, black women's writing imagines the future in the present. It sees the future born out of the context of oppression. It produces utopia out of the transformation of the most basic features of daily life, everything we tend to take for granted.

As black women writers envision it, the utopian transformation of society depends on the radical reconstitution of domestic life and space. The future takes shape within the walls that have traditionally imprisoned women and defined their social labor: the home. Black women's writing does not explode the household nor does it situate the realization of women's potentialities in the workplace. Rather, it works on the commonplace features of daily life, from household objects to household labor, from childbearing to sexuality. It asks how these might be lifted out of the oppressive and repressive constraints defined by bourgeois society and capitalism. It asks how these might be changed and at the same time preserved as the contextual elements of domestic life. In so doing, the fiction lays the basis for expanding its transformed image out of the household and into society at large.

When, at the end of *The Color Purple*, Walker describes Celie's Fourth of July picnic, she fleshes out one of the most prevalent utopian visions in black women's writing. At the heart of this vision is the redefinition of social relationships based on the extended family, whose contours have been stretched into the community by the inclusion of friends, neighbors, and co-workers. Age, sex, wealth, and power do not produce domination among the group's members. Rather, all are bound up in a network of care that is as sustaining and open as the rambling architecture of Celie's "down home" house.

Walker's utopian vision is predicated on the transformation of the two most significant determinants of a woman's domestic life: sexuality and economics. Lesbianism gives Celie the means for transforming her body, previously defined as an object for use, into the site of her pleasure and her means for giving pleasure to another. It transforms her bed and bedroom, previously defined as zones for the reproduction of male domination and the economic expropriation of women, into a context for discovering new bases for social relationships. However, the changes produced by Celie's discovery of self through sexuality would have been stymied and eventually contained had it not been for her simultaneous development of a mode of economic support that, like lesbianism, is also not inscribed within capitalism's dominant forms.

Walker's view of economics is strongly influenced by the rural South. Implicit in Celie's Fourth of July barbecue is the surrounding countryside and the availability of cheap local farm produce and neighborly gifts of food. The lap that cradles Celie's development of an alternative mode of production is the unchanged base of rural agriculture, which is often as brutalizing of its workers as it is life-sustaining for the larger population. The unmentioned agricultural base may well constitute a contradiction for Celie's solution to economic exploitation, which updates cottage-style industry to suit the tastes of postsixties generations.

Seen in microcosm, leaving aside its problematical relationship to larger economic structures, Celie's introduction of artisanal industry into the home achieves the radical transformation of her daily life and living space. Begun in the dining room, Celie's production of custom pants soon spreads its transformative influence, like her sexual relationship with Shug, throughout the house: "Pants all over her chairs, hanging all in front of the china closet. Newspaper patterns and cloth all over the table and the floor. . . ."[2] Reciprocity in love and production crowds out the relics of household space and the routines these normally define. Cottage industry, as Walker portrays it, radically redefines sewing in the home, which, in the traditional male-dominated household, is just one of many domestic tasks whose totality defines the reproduction of domination. For Celie, the production of pants is as gratifying as her discovery of a nondominated form of sexuality, and it establishes a reciprocity of satisfaction between producers and consumers.

Walker's treatment of the transformation of domestic space in *The Color Purple* has its literary antecedent in her first novel, *The Third Life of Grange Copeland*. Both novels are similar in their understanding of how all economic accumulation is predicated on the brutal oppression of women and the expropriation of women's productive and reproductive labor. Both novels depict the nuclear family as the primary site of exploitation under capitalism and male domination. Where the novels diverge is in their realization of the utopian future. Economic transformation in *The Third Life of Grange Copeland* is based totally on a return to the ideal of the rural homestead. The farm Grange Copeland owns outright and bequeathes to his granddaughter defines a form of small-scale, self-contained production, whose ability to satisfy and sustain its members is largely related to the fact that as a production unit, the farm is totally severed from economic chains of supply and demand. In this utopia, harvesting, because it is not destined for the market, assumes the gratuitous pleasure of flower picking and production results in delightful side products. "[Grange] raised his own bread, fermented his own wine, cured his own meat. At last he was free" (*TLGC*, 156).

Because the farm, as Grange and Ruth work it and live on it, is not inscribed within the usual contingencies of rural production, it creates a space for the fulfillment of their personal relationship and the transformation of the domestic space they share. Because Ruth is not Grange's wife, lover, or even his daughter, but his granddaughter, she does not fit into any of the typical male-dominated patterns that define the way men live with women. Neither the interior decor nor the objects of their daily life assume the same meanings they would have in a nuclear-family setting. Rather, the rooms and their furnishings give sensual delight. "Ruth's room was a veritable sun of brightness and yellow and white" (*TLGC*, 197). As in *The Color Purple*, color is a sign for the discovery and recovery of sensual pleasure in human relationships. "Grange's room was all in brown and red and blue and black" (*TLGC*, 197). In this domestic space, the separate color schemes do not suggest residues of sexist determinants as they would in a bourgeois household where boys' rooms and clothes are supposed to be blue while little girls get stuck with pink. Rather, color gives resonance to the smells and textures of the objects that define each person's mode of dress and habits, such as Grange's tobacco, flannel underwear, and heavy brogans. This is very different from the bourgeois households we find in novels by Marshall and Morrison, where oak tables, silver, and dark interiors indicate the occupant's class standing. The object relationships Walker describes in her utopian households do not crowd out the people nor do they submerge them under their preponderant weight. Rather, they speak for mutuality in human relationships and the rewarding use of domestic space.

Walker is not the only black woman writer today whose utopian vision is based on return to the South and the resurrection of the homestead. Marshall's *Praisesong for the Widow* concludes with the same image of rambling house and extended household relationships we find in *The Color Purple*. So, too, is Marshall's sense of alternative social relationships predicated on the same sort of redefinition of the family we find in *The Third Life of Grange Copeland*. Instead of the grandfather-granddaughter homestead, Marshall envisions a household nucleus composed of grandmother and grandchildren, whose familial component is then expanded by the addition of many more children—all of whom would transform the house into a summer camp. The notion of a camp highlights the desire to evolve a space for living and working that neither reproduces this society's social relationships nor perpetuates its exploitative economic modes. In imagining an offshore island as the site of the summer camp, Marshall demonstrates the need for creating distance from American economic hegemony and bourgeois cultural domination, while at the same time still being identified as American and representing an American possibility. Marshall's summer camp articulates the desire to bring about transformation at the level of the close-at-hand and doable; it also shows the limitations involved when the imaginative space for transformation is not given access to a larger field of possibility.

As in all aspects of contemporary black women's fiction, the voice of Hurston haunts these images of the future. The imagined households Marshall and Walker describe may well have had their literary inspiration in Hurston's description of her own childhood home:

> We had oranges, tangerines and grapefruit to use as hand-grenades on the neighbor's children. . . .
> Our house had eight rooms, and we called it a two-story house; but later on I learned it was really one story and a jump. The big boys all slept up there, and it was a good place to hide and shirk from sweeping off the front porch or raking up the back yard.

Downstairs in the dining-room there was an old "safe," a punched design in its tin doors. Glasses of guava jelly, quart jars of pear, peach and other kinds of preserves. The left over cooked foods were on the lower shelves.

There were eight children in the family, and our house was noisy from the time school turned out until bedtime. (*DT*, 27)

The passage situates the house in the context of rural production, allowing us to imagine the house and its citrus-filled yard as extensions of a larger agricultural domain. Because farm production itself isn't made visible, its products (the oranges and tangerines for throwing) and the canning and cooking related to farm production are all felt to be pleasurable. The house itself suggests both spaciousness and closure, rambling openness and the possibility for solitude.

Whether or not Hurston's real childhood home achieved such a utopian relationship to the rural economy and to its definition of social space is not at issue. The important feature here is the function of childhood memory, which creates the same valuable distance between the writer and the fabric of social and economic relationships that Marshall and Walker attain when they project their images for future society back into past economic modes. As Hurston remembers the domestic space she perceived through the eyes of childhood, she captures an image of a household that is lifted out of the economic and social constraints she would have clearly seen if she looked on the same scene with the eyes of an adult. Childhood is the mode of utopian realization. It transforms work into play and closure into freedom as easily as Hurston as a child transformed a bar of soap and a corn husk into "Mr. Sweet Smell" and "Miss Corn-Shuck" (*DT*, 73).

By far the most radical image of the utopian transformation of social relationships comes from a writer whose public political life does not include the left orientations we associate with Bambara and Walker. Nevertheless, the transformative images of domestic life we find in Morrison's first three novels are so striking and offer such far-reaching implications for the redefinition of human social relationships that they make Morrison one of the great utopian visionaries. When the child Pecola, so brow-beaten and racially inferiorized as to believe herself just plain "ugly" (*TBE*, 34), flees her family's storefront apartment and seeks out her upstairs neighbors, she enters a world whose decor and occupants may look like the novel's 1940s setting, but whose social space and relationships embody future aspirations. The antithesis between the novels' two worlds could not be more sharply drawn. Morrison describes the nuclear family—not its bourgeois ideal depicted in the passage from the "Dick and Jane" reader that opens the novel, but the nuclear family as it has en-hanced the grim despair and brutal dehumanization of black people living in poverty. For the Breedloves, living as a family is synonymous with reproducing the social forms of the system of their impoverishment. Pecola's mother, ground down by toil and disillusionment, has been robbed of the pleasures of childbear-ing for the sake of rearing her white employer's children. Pecola's father, blindly and violently domineering, enacts the frustration of unemployment and alcoholism on the bodies of his wife and children. Pecola herself and her brother—what dreams might they have? what feelings? what futures? The only positive thing we might say about Pecola's tragic end is that the cancellation of her future includes, by way of negation, the wished-for end of the nuclear family.

The antithesis of the nuclear family is Morrison's three-woman household. In *The Bluest Eye* the three-woman house-hold is composed of three prostitutes. In *Song of Solomon* and *Sula* the relationships are familial and generational. What mat-ters is not the variety of circumstances that might bring three women together, but the way their being together produces the radical transformation of domestic space. What Pecola hears when she runs to the upstairs apartment is "Poland singing—her voice sweet and hard, like new strawberries" (*TBE*, 43). Rather than her father's drunken snores, her mother's enraged silence, and, finally, their violent outbursts, Pecola hears womanly banter: "Hi, dumplin'. Where your socks" (*TBE*, 46). Giggles, chuckles and provocative exclamations fill the interior with the same spontaneous disarray as the prostitutes' hair curlers and brassieres. While the women's activities—ironing, dressing, and fixing their hair—represent a form of domestic labor geared for their function as prostitutes, nothing that the women do inside their domestic space or in relation to each other (or Pecola) is defined by male domination. This is in strong contrast to the way all women's activity in the nuclear family redounds in the male domination of the household.

Significantly, all of Morrison's three-woman households are composed of heterosexual women. In refusing to confront male domination on the basis of lesbianism, Morrison develops the critical potential of female heterosexuality. For the most part, the women in the households continue to have sexual relationships with men, but men do not define the way they live their lives. Rather than the mode and means of a woman's oppression, heterosexuality becomes the basis for establishing a critical tension between the household and society at large.

Perhaps the most remarkable three-woman household in Morrison's writing is Eva Peace's boardinghouse. Its spontaneous architecture—some rooms giving only on to porches, "private" rooms that must be crossed in order to get to more public ones, multiple stairways, porches, and alcoves—recapitulates the desire for a rambling, nonclaustrophobic domestic space. The occupants of Eva Peace's house are as heterogeneous as its floor plan. Its three-woman core, composed of Eva, her daughter, her granddaughter, is fleshed out by a steady supply of boarders, adopted children, and a host of male visitors. Although Eva might be said to "preside" over the household, she does not dominate. Nor is domestic activity defined by a prescribed division of labor, sexual or otherwise.

Finally, the economic underpinnings of Eva Peace's household are far more contestatory of capitalism than the notion of a return to either homestead or artisanal industry we find elsewhere in black women's utopian visions. The boardinghouse and its three-woman nucleus are predicated on Eva's radical manipulation of the corporate enterprise system. When, destitute and abandoned, Eva allowed a train to run over and sever her leg, she performed the first stage of the revolutionary transformation of her life. Eva's act is not self-destructive, but self-affirming, for it is with the railroad company's insurance money that Eva builds her home, dedicated to the transformation of the American Dream.

Nevertheless, it is interesting to note that residues of the rural utopian image inform Morrison's three-woman households and suggest that the ties to the rural South and the agricultural base have not been broken. Pilate's household in *Song of Solomon* is the most rural in its definition of domestic labor. Even though her production of wine is not for profit and the organization of household economics is devoted to nonaccumulation, Pilate's life-style suggests the familiar constraints of home farming in her tendency to eat whatever is in season and nothing else, be it peaches, corn, or berries. All of Morrison's three-woman households depict continuity with rural production in their images of canning, shelves stocked with summer preserves, the big stewpot in the yard. Even the prostitutes in *The Bluest Eye* evoke the rural South when they summon up memories of fried fish— caught, cooked, and eaten on the spot right down to the lip-smacking taste and sticky fingers.

What's most important in all these attempts to envision alternative futures out of the past's range of possibilities are the tangibly different people and relationships that emerge once capitalism's constraints give way to the utopian imagination. We as readers experience along with Macon Dead the uplifting fascination of peering through a window into utopia. The world outside is profit motivated and people exploitative; it transforms cultures of vitality into cults of the commodity; and it reduces sexuality to domination and repression. In contrast, the world inside privileges people over profits, domestic activity over labor, and spontaneous consumption over routine. This is the world we see as we look over Macon Dead's shoulder into the house that Toni Morrison built on the principles of potlatch and reciprocity.

Childhood relived from the point of view of an adult is very often the mode of utopian realization. And the commonplace, once disassociated from bourgeois society, becomes the ground for alternative imagination. As women, the writers discussed in this book are sublimely in touch with both possibilities. As black women, they have felt all the more the crucial importance of transforming the future.

Notes
Bibliograpic Note
Index

Notes

Chapter 1.   Histories, Communities, and Sometimes Utopia

1   I feel that the only way to develop a theoretical approach to the work of contemporary black women writers is to define their writing in relation to a history larger than the personal and literary. Moreover, I suggest that the sense of history that shapes black women's writing is larger and more profound than one specifically determined by race and culture.

2   Toni Morrison, *The Bluest Eye* (New York: Pocket Books, 1972), 67. Hereafter cited as *TBE*.

3   Paule Marshall, *Brown Girl, Brownstones* (Old Westbury, N.Y.: The Feminist Press, 1981), 192. Hereafter cited as *BGB*.

4   See Historical Statistics of the United States Colonial Times to 1970 (Washington, D.C.: US Department of Commerce, Bureau of the Census, 1976), 139.

5   The notion that the conquest of the New World took place in a world economic system already defined by capitalism is one of the basic tenets of dependency economic theory. See Immanuel Wallerstein, *The Modern World System* (New York: Academic Press, 1974).

6   Alice Walker, *In Search of Our Mothers' Gardens* (New York: Harcourt Brace Jovanovich, 1983), 231–43.

7   Alice Walker, *The Third Life of Grange Copeland* (New York: Harcourt Brace Jovanovich, 1977). Hereafter cited as *TLGC*.

8   LeRoi Jones, *Blues People* (New York: William Morrow, 1965).

9   "Buy house" reverberates throughout *Brown Girl, Brownstones*, where it encapsulates the Barbadians' ardent desire for integration into the American system.

171

10 Toni Morrison, *Song of Solomon* (New York: New American Library, 1977). Hereafter cited as *SOS*.

11 Zora Neale Hurston, *Dust Tracks on the Road* (New York: Arno Press and the New York Times, 1969), 195. Hereafter cited as *DT*.

12 LeRoi Jones, *Blues People*, 28.

13 George Lamming's remarks come out of a conversation I had with the author at Yale University in the spring of 1981. We were discussing the relationship of his most allegorical novel, *Natives of My Person*, to his other novels.

14 Fredric Jameson developed the significance of allegory at the Robert C. Elliot Memorial Lecture, University of California, San Diego, April 1985.

15 Sigmund Freud, "The Interpretation of Dreams," in *The Standard Edition of the Complete Works of Sigmund Freud*, trans. James Strachey (London: Hogarth Press, 1973), 277–304.

16 See Susan Willis, "Aesthetics of the Rural Slum: Contradictions and Dependency in 'The Bear' " in *Faulkner (New Perspectives)*, ed. Richard Brodhead (Englewood Cliffs, N.J.: Prentice-Hall, 1983), 174–94.

17 Nicolas Guillén, *Man-Making Words* (Amherst: Univ. of Massachusetts Press, 1972), 19.

18 Ibid, 21.

19 Ibid, 19.

20 Georg Lukács, *The Historical Novel* (Boston: Beacon Press, 1962), 39.

21 Ibid, 33.

22 Ibid, 36.

23 Ibid, 36.

Chapter 2.   Wandering

1 Zora Neale Hurston, *Mules and Men* (Bloomington: Indiana Univ. Press, 1978), 4. Hereafter cited as *MM*.

2 Zora Neale Hurston, *Their Eyes Were Watching God* (Urbana: Univ. of Illinois Press, 1978), 37. Hereafter cited as *EWW*.

3 Harriette Arnow, *The Dollmaker* (New York: Macmillan, 1954).

4 The Cuban slave poet, Juan Francisco Manzano, was one such writer, who, in entrusting his narrative to an English abolitionist, had little assurance that it ever would be published or that he might one day hold his own autobiography in his hands. For a fuller account of Manzano's narrative and the difficulties sur-

rounding his life as a writer, see Susan Willis, "Crushed Geraniums: Juan Francisco Manzano and the Language of Slavery," in *The Slave's Narrative*, ed. Charles T. Davis and Henry Louis Gates, Jr. (New York: Oxford Univ. Press, 1985), 199–224.

5 Amos Tutuola, *The Palm-Wine Drinkard* (New York: Grove, 1953).

6 Hurston makes many comparisons between the plight of rural black women and animals; in *Their Eyes Were Watching God*, she says: "De nigger woman is de mule uh de world so fur as Ah can see" (*EWW*, 29). I feel that the disparity between the strong, positive portrayal of women in the folktales and the potentially demeaning connotations of their comparison with mules, which the title *Mules and Men* cannot help but suggest, represents another of Hurston's backhanded and subtle attempts to undermine prevailing ideology. It should be noted that there are very few mules in the stories and a great number of assertive women—both in the tales and as tale-tellers.

7 This is the basis for the political aesthetic of negritude poetry as Sartre describes it in his essay, "Orphée Noire," (originally published as the preface to *Anthologie de la nouvelle poésie nègre et malgache de langue française* by L. Sédar Senghor (Presses Universitaires de France, 1948). What differentiates the poetry of such writers as Léopold Sédar Senghor and Aimé Césaire from the Afro-American tale-telling tradition is that the negritude poets are writing in a very literary and sophisticated form of French while the tale-tellers are working in the oral dialect. As Sartre sees it, when black people rise up and speak—and do so in the language of their oppressor—their act so reverses domination as to put an end to racist society. Extrapolating from Sartre's logic, we might say that the failure of the folktales to be transformative of society resides in their use of dialect and, therefore, their perpetuation of a culture of otherness.

8 In his masterful novel, *Things Fall Apart*, Chinua Achebe describes the last years of traditional, village-based African culture. As he depicts the process of a child's growing up and acculturation, Achebe mentions that as boys enter adolescence they begin to spend more time with their fathers, who narrate very different stories from the ones their mothers would tell—and will go on telling to their girl children. It seems that women's stories pertain to the world of myth—the animal heroes, origins, and cosmology—whereas the men's stories pertain to the world of history—events like battles and tribal genealogy. As the story of

Jack and the Devil makes clear, the Afro-American stories com-
press myth and history. It may well be that when the plantation
system leveled the traditional African division of labor, which defined men as hunters and warriors and women as planters, food
preparers, and child raisers, it created a situation in which the distinction between a male and a female discourse no longer obtained. If this is so, the roots of the great American mythic novel
(Gabriel García Marquez's *Cien Años de Soledad*) (New York:
Avon, 1971) may reside in the combination of myth and history
that we find in the Afro-American stories.

9   In her description of Joe Starks, Hurston is paraphrasing the real
history of her hometown, Eatonville, and its founding father, Joe
Clarke. For her account of Eatonville's inception, see the chapter
called "My Birthplace" in *Dust Tracks on a Road*.

Chapter 3.   Describing Arcs of Recovery

1   Paule Marshall, *Praisesong for the Widow* (New York: G. P. Put-
nam's Sons, 1983). Hereafter cited as *PS*.

> I wanted to know my mother when she sat
> looking sad across the campus in the late 20's
> into the future of the soul, there were black angels
> straining above her head, carrying life from the ancestors,
> and knowledge, and the strong nigger feeling. . . .
>
> —Amiri Baraka

2   Octavia E. Butler, *Kindred* (New York: Pocket Books, 1981).

3   Walter Benjamin, "The Storyteller," in *Illuminations* (New York:
Schocken Books, 1976), 83–109.

4   The history of maroon societies (formed by escaped slaves) functions as a symbol for liberation throughout Afro-American writing. For a description of maroon culture and social organization,
see Richard Price, *Maroon Societies: Rebel Slave Communities in
the Americas* (Baltimore: Johns Hopkins University Press, 1979).

5   Jean Toomer, *Cane* (New York: Harper & Row, 1968), 88.

Chapter 4.   Eruptions of Funk

1   Much of the criticism of Morrison's work is done from a sociolog-
ical point of view. See, for example, Joan Bischoff, "The Novels of
Toni Morrison: Studies in Thwarted Sensitivity," Studies in Black
Literature 6, 3 (1975): 21–23; Phyllis Klotman, "Dick-and-Jane
and the Shirley Temple Sensibility in *The Bluest Eye*," *Black*

American Literature Forum 13 (1979): 123–25; Barbara Louns-
berry and Grace Anne Hovet, "Principles of Perception in Toni
Morrison's *Sula,*" *Black American Literature Forum* 13 (1979):
126–29. These studies focus on the erosion of the individual's
sensitivity by white cultural domination, on the one hand, and
ordering mechanisms within the black neighborhood on the
other. The critics tend to agree that, although Morrison regrets
the loss of sensitivity, she favors a practical and pragmatic point
of view.

Without denying the objective social fact or the importance of
literary studies that document the social in literature, I am more
interested in how texts subvert the limitations within which they
are written. The focus of this study is, thus, on those instances in
Morrison's writing in which the literature does something more
than simply monitor and confirm social fact.

2   The surrealist metaphors of the negritude poets resist being read
in the way we can read through Morrison's metaphors, progres-
sively constructing their referents and meaning. An example from
Aimé Césaire's *Cahier d'un Retour au Pays Natal* in *Aimé Césaire,*
trans. Clayton Eshleman and Annette Smith (Berkeley: Univ. of
California Press, 1983) exemplifies the difference between the poetics of negritude and Morrison's use of metaphor.

Conjuring up the Congo, Césaire depicts a rich natural setting:

> où l'eau fait
> likouala—likouala (p. 50)

"Where the water goes likouala—likouala." This is followed by
one of the most complex and condensed examples of surrealist
metaphor:

> où l'éclair de la colère lance sa hache verdâtre
> et force les sangliers de la putréfaction dans
> la belle orée violente des narines (p. 50)

Reading the metaphor produces something like this: "Where the
lightning bolt of anger hurls its green ax and forces the wild boars
of putrefaction over the beautiful and violent edge of the nostrils."

Overall, the image evokes the powerful and driving force of nature and the hunt. Individual words are themselves metaphors,
linked together to form a total metaphoric image whose meaning
does not reside in a particular referent, but in the myriad cross-
references pulled into the whole.

The "lightning bolt of anger" captures the essence of the poem
as a whole, for it voices the enraged outcry of black people and reverses the image of the meek, long-suffering "comical and ugly

nigger" ("un nègre comique et laid," 62–63) produced by colonialism. The image of "wild boars pouring over the nostrils" (like snot) extends the notion of putrefaction, which is itself a code word for the effects of colonialism. This is developed at length in the poem's opening pages where the Antilles are portrayed not as a tropical island paradise but as a degraded, diseased, and decayed speck of land:

> Ici la parade des risibles et scrofuleux bubons, les poutures des microbes très étranges, les poisons sans alexitère connu, les sanies de plaies bien antiques, les fermentations imprévisibles d'éspèces putrescibles. (p. 38)

> Right here the parade of laughable and scrofulous buboes, the forced feedings of very strange microbes, the poisons without known alexins, the sanies of really ancient sores, the unforeseeable fermentations of putrescible species. (p. 39)

Bodily orifices, too, are in more than one instance related to the visage of colonialism. But these observations do not translate what the metaphor says; rather, they are embraced by it. There is no single, comprehensive way to decipher Césaire's metaphor as there is for Morrison's. This is because, although history infuses the image, the metaphor resists being tied to any specific referent or set of referents. The effect is finally an explosion of meanings, created out of the convergence of many possible interpretations, as opposed to Morrison's revelation of meaning, made possible by linking images to referents.

3   Harriette Arnow's *The Dollmaker* (New York: Avon, 1973), an account of an Appalachian family's migration to Detroit during World War II, is very similar to Morrison's portrayal of black Southern migration. Notably, it documents the initial experience and assimilation to wage labor, the erosion of folk culture, and the fragmentation of the family unit. In Arnow as in Morrison, the individual's experience of alienation is portrayed in relation to fetishization under the commodity form. For a brief discussion of *The Dollmaker*, see Susan Willis, "A Literary Lesson in Historical Thinking," *Social Text*, no. 3 (1980): 136ff.

4   See Georg Lukács, "Reification and the Consciousness of the Proletariat," in *History and Class Consciousness* (London: Merlin Press, 1971), 83. According to Lukács, reification occurs when the "commodity structure penetrates society in all its aspects and remoulds it in its own image" (p. 85). This differentiates bourgeois society from previous social modes, in which the commodity

form may have pertained to certain endeavors or may have been only partially developed. Reification means the transformation of all human functions and qualities into commodities "and reveals in all its starkness the dehumanized and dehumanizing function of the commodity relation" (p. 92).

5   Referred to as "The Principal Beauty of Maine," Margaret Lenore from *Tar Baby* (New York: Knopf, 1981), 11, comes closest to embodying bourgeois reification. Her characterization may well be a literary allusion to another great beauty and bourgeois stereotype in contemporary fiction: "The Most Beautiful Woman in the World," in Gabriel García Marquez's *One Hundred Years of Solitude* (New York: Avon, 1971), 192. Both Margaret Lenore and Marquez's "Most Beautiful Woman" are first beheld by their future husbands as beauty-contest winners in a parade and draped in ermine. However, neither Margaret Lenore nor Marquez's Fernanda define total reification. First of all, neither is originally of the bourgeois class: Fernanda is the sole survivor of a transplanted and bankrupt Spanish aristocracy and Margaret Lenore is the daughter of struggling Italian immigrants. Both develop forms of hysteria as a result of the discontinuity between their pasts and presents and their imperfect assimilation into bourgeois culture. Margaret Lenore abuses her infant son and Fernanda develops a relationship with imaginary doctors she hopes will cure her bodily ailments through telepathic surgery (a situation not unlike Margaret Lenore's long-distance telephone conservations with her son, which, because no one witnesses or overhears them, appear to be imaginary).

6   In Morrison's writing, candy is often associated with capitalism. In *Song of Solomon*, candy is the symbolic payoff given by the boss's wife when Guitar's father is crushed in a mill accident. In *The Bluest Eye*, candy is a penny's worth of sweetness in the life of a little girl who will never find satisfaction in human terms. And in *Tar Baby*, candy is a metaphor for all of capitalist production. The association is not gratuitous, for the connection between candy and capitalism extends far beyond the current glut of sugary breakfast cereals and junk foods. As Immanuel Wallerstein explains in *The Modern World System*, (New York: Academic Press, 1974) sugar production in the New World was essential to the rise of capitalism. Rather than simply satisfying luxury consumption, a lot of the sugar produced under slavery in the Caribbean found its way into the daily diet of the growing European proletariat. With many peasants leaving the countryside to seek

jobs in the cities, there was an increased need for food production and a shrinking rural labor force. The need for more food was met neither by increased cereal production (which would have required substantial transformations in production techniques) nor by increasing meat production (which was basically intended for the bourgeoisie). Rather, sugar became—and remains today—a substitute for real food. Capable of providing increased energy output at the expense of long-term health, sugar is the opiate of the working class under capitalism. See also Sidney Mintz, *Sweetness and Power* (New York: Viking, 1985).

7   Toni Morrison, *Tar Baby* (New York: Knopf, 1981), 61. Hereafter cited as *TB*.

8   Toni Morrison, *Sula* (New York: Knopf, 1974), 3. Hereafter cited as *S*.

9   Abandoned at birth by his mother, rejected by his father for the sake of a poker game, and having experienced the ultimate moment of objectification when two white hunters catch him in his first sex act, Cholly Breedlove finds absolute freedom in the realization that he has nothing to lose. In many ways he is Pilate's antithesis, his freedom being a barrier rather than a bridge to others. Unlike Pilate, who similarly did not know her mother's name, who lost her father, and also experienced the freezing "look" of others for her lack of a navel, Cholly can neither communicate nor share his freedom.

10 Many modernist novels from the Third World include "mythic heroes" very similar to Faulkner's Thomas Sutpen. In Mario Vargas Llosa's *The Green House* (New York: Avon, 1973), Don Anselmo bursts upon a stodgy, backwater town, shrouded in mystery, apparently without a past or a name. Like Sutpen, he embarks on an enterprise that the townspeople marvel at and at first do not comprehend. What Don Anselmo builds symbolizes exploitation in the Third World: a brothel. The "mythic hero" creates a distance from society, which produces an estrangement effect and reveals that what was first perceived as very different and foreign is nothing more than that society's ultimate representation.

11 The otherness of blindness and the fear it instills in a repressive bourgeois society are developed in *Sobre Héroes y Tumbas*, (Buenos Aires: Editorial Losada, 1966), the great historical novel by the Argentinian Ernesto Sábato. Similar to Morrison's portrayal, Sábato conjures up an underground society of the blind whose otherness, perceived as grotesque from the point of view of

the Peronist social model, is the basis for the group's solidarity and resistance to assimilation by the forces of domination.

12 The relationship between forms of mutilation and freedom is not unique to Morrison, but recurs in the history of slavery and its literature. In his mythic account of the Haitian Revolution, *The Kingdom of This World* (New York: Collier, 1970), Alejo Carpentier portrays the mutilation of Mackandal, an early slave leader, in terms that coincide with Morrison's treatment. His arm crushed in a cane mill and amputated, Mackandal is unfit for most forms of plantation labor. Freed from the most grueling forms of toil, he wanders the countryside watching over his master's livestock. There he discovers and studies plant and animal life, learning the secrets of science and voodoo. Mutilation is thus the means for Mackandal's liberation from labor and access to learning. Furthermore, because Mackandal, as voodoo priest, is capable of undergoing various metamorphoses, his human body and its mutilation are not perceived as permanently disabled, but rather, as one more manifestation of transitory and transitional matter. Mackandal's spiritual liberation—made possible by his mutilation—finally transcends his earthy form.

13 William Faulkner, *Absalom! Absalom!* (1936; rpt. New York: Random House, 1972), 155.

Chapter 5. Alice Walker's Women

1 Alice Walker, *Revolutionary Petunias and Other Poems* (New York: Harcourt Brace Jovanovich, 1973), 31.

2 Alice Walker, *In Search of Our Mothers' Gardens* (New York: Harcourt Brace Jovanovich, 1983), 17.

3 See introductory discussion and previous chapter on Toni Morrison.

4 Alice Walker, *Meridian* (New York: Pocket Books, 1977), 31. Hereafter cited as *M*.

5 As a negative qualification, I wish to add that the possibility for transformation in *The Third Life of Grange Copeland* is based on the toil and abuse of three women personally connected with Grange, who stand in something of a generational relationship to each other: Margaret, Grange's wife, whom he abandons; Mem, Grange's daughter-in-law, who is murdered by her husband (Grange's son); and Josie, Grange's mistress, whom he jilts and bilks. It is only by the accumulation of their labor and misery that Grange is able to break the chains that bind him to the enslave-

ment of sharecropping. So Ruth's future will bear the burden of the women who toiled and died for her possibilities.

6 John Neihardt, *Black Elk Speaks*, (New York: Pocket Books, 1972), 35.

7 The category of "bitch" is highly contradictory in that it articulates two widely divergent black male fantasies regarding white women. On the one hand, Lynne is perceived as a paragon of domestic virtue, cooking and sewing for the Civil Rights workers; on the other hand, she is perceived as a wanton libertine who asks for and deserves to be raped. Because rape cannot be thought of in isolation, but must be understood in relation to the black male fear of lynching, the entire complex of meanings associated with the category "bitch" would seem to derive not from black male sexual fantasies alone, but from the way these have been conditioned by dominant white male sexuality and political oppression.

8 Literacy has always been linked to liberation in the history of black writing. When Frederick Douglass's mistress begins to teach the alphabet to her young slave, she is roundly scolded by her husband, who says, "if you give a nigger an inch, he will take an ell" (p. 49); "he would know nothing but the will of his master, and learn to obey it" (p. 49). "Learning will spoil the best nigger in the world" (p. 49); "if you teach that nigger [speaking of Douglass] how to read there will be no keeping him" (p. 49); "it would forever unfit him to be a slave"; "if you teach him how to read, he'll want to know how to write; and this accomplished, he'll be running away with himself" (Frederick Douglass, *Narrative of the Life of Frederick Douglass* [New York: New American Library, 1968], 49).

Douglass takes his master's words to heart, clearly seeing that his struggle for liberation must begin with the mastery of his master's written language:

> The effect of his words, on me, was neither slight or transitory. His iron sentences—cold and harsh—sunk deep into my heart, and stirred up not only my feelings into a sort of rebellion, but awakened within me a slumbering train of vital thought. It was a new and special revelation, dispelling a painful mystery, against which my youthful understanding had struggled, and struggled in vain, to wit: the white man's power to perpetuate the enslavement of the black man. (Douglass, *Narrative of the Life of Frederick Douglass*, 49).

Chapter 6. Problematizing the Individual

1 Toni Cade Bambara, *The Salt Eaters* (New York: Random House, 1980). Hereafter cited as *SE*.

2 Toni Cade Bambara, *The Sea Birds Are Still Alive* (New York: Random House, 1982), 45. Hereafter cited as *SB*.

3 Toni Cade Bambara, *Gorilla, My Love* (New York: Random House, 1972). Hereafter cited as *GML*.

4 To define a dramatic reversal of the "mud mothers" and their cave paintings, I call your attention to Judy Baca and the stunning mural paintings she has done in and around Los Angeles. In taking art to the ghetto, the freeways, and the flood-control channels, she has made art public. In teaching unemployed teenagers, who, in fact, do most of the painting, she has created a community of artists.

5 Edward Said, in *The World, the Text, and the Critic* (Cambridge: Harvard Univ. Press, 1983) defines the inception of modernism in Western culture in terms of a transition from relationships of filiation to those of affiliation. As he puts it:

> Childless couples, orphaned children, aborted childbirths, and unregeneratedly celibate men and women populate the world of high modernism with remarkable insistence, all of them suggesting the difficulties of filiation. But no less important in my opinion is the second part of the pattern, which is immediately consequent upon the first, the pressure to produce new and different ways of conceiving human relationships. For if biological reproduction is either too difficult or too unpleasant, is there some other way by which men and women can create social bonds between each other that would substitute for those ties that connect members of the same family across generations? (p. 17).

Bambara's writing spans such a transition and grapples with the problem of how to define human social relationships, once the form of the family has been transcended.

Chapter 7. Envisioning the Future

1 Marge Piercy, *Woman on the Edge of Time* (New York: Fawcett, 1976).

2 Alice Walker, *The Color Purple* (New York: Harcourt Brace Jovanovich, 1982), 180.

Bibliographic Note

The following books are listed because they develop either feminism or literary criticism from the point of view of black women. (A number of the texts work in both areas.) Some of the books are more basic than others; some are demanding, some provocative. A few of the texts are comprehensive; others focus on specific issues. Some are challenging and suggest new areas for thought and criticism; others employ established methods and demonstrate how these either suceed or fail in the analysis of black women's history and writing. Taken as a whole, these books define the critical context for my thinking about the literature. None of these texts is directly cited in my interpretations because I chose not to speak to the criticism. Such a method would have produced a very different book. Rather, my aim has been to concentrate on writing by black women, with the criticism something of an overall framework for my observations.

I've listed books as a way of defining an accessible and available body of readings. There are, however, two important articles that I mention to round out the book-length discussions and collections that appear below. Both are devoted to rethinking the literature by women in terms of a lesbian perspective. Of these, Barbara Smith's interpretation of Morrison's *Sula* has stimulated both controversy and fruitful debate (Barbara Smith, "Towards a Black Feminist Criticism," *Conditions Two* 1 (October 1977). Smith's essay should be read along with Bonnie Zimmerman's larger study of women's writing, reassessing it against a male-defined literary canon and in relation to a lesbian feminist tradition (Bonnie Zimmerman, "What Has Never Been: An Overview of Lesbian Feminist Criticism," in *Making a Difference*, ed. Gayle Green and Coppélia Kahn [London: Methuen, 1985]).

Bell, Roseann P., Bettye J. Parker, and Beverly Guy-Sheftall, eds. *Sturdy Black Bridges*. New York: Doubleday, 1979.

Christian, Barbara. *Black Women Novelists: The Development of a Tradition, 1892–1976*. Westport, Conn.: Greenwood Press, 1980.

Christian, Barbara. *Black Feminist Criticism: Perspectives on Black Women Writers*. New York: Pergamon Press, 1986.

Davis, Angela. *Women, Race and Class*. New York: Random House, 1981.

Evans, Mari, ed. *Black Women Writers*. New York: Doubleday, 1984.

Gates, Henry Louis, Jr., ed. *Black Literature and Literary Theory*. London: Methuen, 1984.

Hooks, Bell. *Ain't I a Woman*. Boston: South End Press, 1982.

Hooks, Bell. *Feminist Theory: From Margin to Center*. Boston: South End Press, 1984.

Hull, Gloria T., Patricia Bell Scott, and Barbara Smith, eds. *All the Women Are White, All the Blacks Are Men, But Some of Us Are Brave: Black Women's Studies*. Old Westbury, N.Y.: Feminist Press, 1982.

Lerner, Gerda. *Black Women in White America*. New York: Random House, 1972.

Lorde, Audre. *Sister Outsider*. New York: Crossing Press, 1984.

Moraga, Cherríe, and Gloria Anzaldúa, eds. *This Bridge Called My Back: Writings by Radical Women of Color*. Watertown, Mass.: Persephone Press, 1981.

Rich, Adrienne. *Of Woman Born*. New York: Norton, 1976.

Smith, Barbara. *Home Girls*. New York: Kitchen Table, Women of Color Press, 1983.

Snitow, Ann, Christine Stansell, and Sharon Thompson, eds. *Powers of Desire*. New York: Monthly Review Press, 1983.

Wallace, Michele. *Black Macho and the Myth of Super Woman*. New York: Dial Press, 1978.

Index

DESIGNED BY JOANNA HILL
COMPOSED BY POINT WEST TYPESETTING
CAROL STREAM, ILLINOIS
MANUFACTURED BY EDWARDS BROTHERS, INC.
ANN ARBOR, MICHIGAN
TEXT AND DISPLAY LINES ARE SET IN TRUMP MEDIAEVAL

ⱳ

Library of Congress Cataloging-in-Publication Data
Willis, Susan.
Specifying: Black women writing the American experience.
(The Wisconsin project on American writers)
Bibliography: pp. 183–184.
Includes index.
1. American fiction—Afro-American authors—History
and criticism.   2. American fiction—Women authors—
History and criticism.   3. American fiction—20th century
—History and criticism.   4. Afro-American women in
literature.   5. Women and literature—United States.
6. History in literature.   7. Literature and history.
8. United States in literature.   I. Title.   II. Series.
PS153.N5W56   1987   813'.5'099287   86-20202
ISBN 0-299-10890-2